For the Love of Lemons

*For all the lemon lovers
of the world, beginning
with my mum.*

For the Love of Lemons

Letitia Clark

Italian-inspired, sweet & savoury recipes

Quadrille

Contents

Love At First Lemon 6

Lost in Lemons 14

One: Salted Lemons 35

Two: Lost in Leaves 107

Three: Sweet Lemons 119

**Four: A Squeeze
of Lemon** 195

Five: Lemon Drops 215

Six: Lemon Jars 231

About the Author 244

Acknowledgements 246

Index 248

LOVE
AT
FIRST
Lemon

The very first lemon I fell in love with was made of plastic. It sported a perfect teat at one end, a tiny, click-shut lid at the other and was dotted all over with perfect dimples. It lived on the top shelf of my grandmother's refrigerator and came out for special occasions, or more precisely, prawn cocktail and pancakes. It looked like a child's bath toy, but somehow simultaneously managed to seem the height of sophistication. I remember seeing these lemons lined up on the supermarket shelves, their Jif labels attached, like little yellow soldiers ready to go into battle, flags waving.

The second lemon I fell for came in a transparent wrapper that crackled and left a light white dust on my fingers. It was a sherbet lemon – knobbly outside to mirror a real lemon's texture and with a mouth-puckering, powdery lemon fizz within. These lemons lived in the glove compartment of my dad's car, next to the black-and-white striped Everton Mints.

The third lemon I fell in love with was the first real lemon I met, with its leaf and stalk still attached. It was huge, heavy, elongated, with thick, matte, deeply dimpled skin. It looked like an oil painting and it smelled like paradise and a journey. It came from a company called Natoora that supplied the first restaurant I worked in, and it had come fresh from Italy, via the markets in Milan. This lemon had a colourful sticker on it that I removed and kept in my apron pocket, because it seemed so sunny, its miniature design singing a song of blue and yellow coastlines, on that very grey day in a concrete corner of London's Kensal Town.

This lemon was the beginning of something, though I didn't know it then. Back then, its presence felt simply cheering on a bitter winter's day. But I wasn't the first to have fallen for such a lemon, or for lemons in general. Throughout their history lemons have been treasured and adored for their aesthetics, their medicinal properties, their perfume and their culinary powers. They have inspired poetry, paintings, and paeans, as well as seasoning countless dishes and drinks with their deliciously fragrant zest and delightfully acidic juice. Someone recently told me they found a lemon on the road on the way home from a holiday in Florence. They named it David (after the *David* they had just seen in situ) and smuggled it into their suitcase. Somehow naming a lemon seems perfectly normal behaviour to me. They are the most anthropomorphic of fruits.

When I moved to Italy, I too fell into the inevitable trap of citrus worship: buying lemons by the bag just to look at them; picking, painting and poring over them. I photographed and fondled them, and took them home as gifts in my suitcase, wrapped in little red ribbons like Christingle oranges. At my local market, the vendors learnt to pick out all the ones with the leaves just for me, not knowing why I cared so much, but charitably doing so anyway. To a non-lemon-lander like me, the leaf and stalk were symbolic of a freshness and vicinity that I had been denied in my former life in England. Even now, after seven years in Italy, I still delight at the sight of a lemon, more so a lemon with leaves. And even though we are surrounded by them and everyone has their own trees, I still pick out the biggest and most bulbous at the market and buy them regardless. They act as instant kitchen ornaments, and simply looking at them makes me happy. My little boy, who has his cot half in the kitchen, had a large fresh lemon as his very first toy.

But, I emphasise, it is not just me who is lifted by lemons. Any traveller from colder climes cannot help but be delighted by the sight of bright yellow lemons dangling from glossy green trees. To the northern eye, like mine, attuned to the muted and russet tones of my indigenous apples and pears, the lemon is a thing of almost mocking brightness and jollity – so bold, blatant and exclamatory in its yellowness. When I was a child, if we went on holiday as a family to a land where lemons grew (Cyprus and Italy) my mother would always stop to photograph them, before stooping to gather windfalls and then smuggling them home in her suitcase. Throughout her life she has tried and failed to cultivate her own lemons at home in England. She is not alone in this citrus worship, something I have inherited, and something that writers through the centuries have also documented.

While travelling in lemon-scented Spain in 1905, Virginia Woolf wrote to a friend, 'I am amazed that we should live in England…when we might roll in bliss every moment of the day and sit and drink coffee on a balcony overlooking lemon trees.' Similarly, Danish author Hans Christian Andersen wrote home, 'My God, my God, how unfairly we are treated in the north: here, here is Paradise!'. The lemon, not the apple, seems to be the fruit that inspires the greatest lust. Lemons and lemon trees act as the signifiers of a certain sun-drenched landscape in the romantic imagination, a certain sun-enriched way of life, even. The sight of lemon trees, with their fat, heavy yellow fruit, dangling from shining evergreen branches, is one that is infinitely cheering, and one that somehow promises sunshine even when it is not summer, for lemons (and other citrus) are the only fruit that grows in an Italian winter. In Giuseppe Arcimboldo's seminal seasonal paintings, the face of Winter is barren and bark-covered, but around his neck is a jaunty citrus necklace of an orange and a lemon, which become the focal points of the painting. The sight of citrus on the trees in an Italian midwinter is infallibly uplifting – they act like coloured baubles in the otherwise lacklustre landscape.

Helena Attlee, in her wonderful study of citrus in Italy, writes that 'Nothing can rob Italy of its citrus legacy, its myriad flavours are integral to Italian food,' and that 'Italy's love of citrus is mutual,' given how happily citrus grows here. Even my own tiny lemon tree seems

to thrive despite my neglect. Italian lemons inspire what Attlee calls 'a mixture of rapture and envy that Italy can still provoke in anyone from colder and less romantic countries'.

This idea of romance is one that repeats, through history, like a long strip of lemon rind, underpinning lemony references in both literature and recipes. In Marcella Hazan's wonderful anthology of Italian cooking, she describes a recipe of 'chicken with two lemons', which then became known popularly as 'engagement chicken', after a magazine reader claimed to have been proposed to after her soon-to-be husband took his first bite. Lemons to fall in love with, indeed.

The perfume of lemons has long been used as a natural antidepressant, true aromatherapy, and their cheerful countenances – somehow so human in their perkiness – continue to delight and inspire as they have for centuries. Even the language associated with the citrus fruit is cheering: take the word 'zest', for example, used to describe piquancy in people or situations, derived from the lively lemon skin, *zeste* as it is in French. Lemons are variously described as electric, fresh, optimistic, uplifting, zesty, spritzy, cheerful, sunny, lively. Lemons are synonymous with freshness and optimism, a fact compounded by the sight of a lemon gone bad: blue-tipped and baggy, it emits a cloud of powder when pressed – a small sigh of melancholy. A happy lemon we know is full, pert and perky, and unapologetically, proudly yellow. The shape of a lemon too, reminiscent of a nipple, a breast, ovoid and cup-like when cut, the texture of its skin, both tender and tough, is extraordinary.

From Pablo Neruda's poem, called *A Lemon*, (see last verse opposite), to sweets, to toys, to paintings, to that first beloved Jif lemon of my youth, which, unknown to me, was one of the most important culinary inventions of the 20th century, the lemon has inspired man (and woman) throughout the ages.

A love for lemons is a love for a lifetime, something that can delight and bring deliciousness to every dish and every day, delivering us from dull food and dreary fruit bowls, forever and ever, Amen.

Long live the lemon!

So, while the hand
holds the cut of the lemon,
half a world on a trencher,
the gold of the universe
wells
to your touch:
a cup yellow
with miracles,
a breast and a nipple
perfuming the earth;
a flashing made fruitage,
the diminutive fire
of a planet.

LOST
IN
Lemons

A Squeeze of History

Man's love affair with lemons is centuries-old, and the modern-day lemon's trajectory from conception to consumption spans most of the world. The small, suspiciously smooth and near-spherical, canary-yellow citrus we find piled up in our supermarkets, peering from our refrigerators and perched in our fruit bowls has had quite the journey to get there. Eyeing a lemon in the hand, cheerful and childlike as it is, one would never guess all that had gone before it.

UNLIKELY ORIGINS: THE CITRON

The modern lemon is most likely derived from a hybrid of citron (what the Italians call *cedro*, which is still found and used in certain recipes today) and a bitter orange, which was itself a hybrid of pomelo and mandarin. All forms of citrus fruits we know today are hybrids derived from the original three naturally occurring species: pomelo, mandarin and citron. These are believed to have come into being around 20 million years ago. Citron was the first citrus fruit known to be cultivated in Europe. Probably first cultivated in India or China, around 2200 BCE, it is not known how it was brought to Europe, though most theories involve Alexander the Great's army, travelling to Macedonia from Persia, carrying citron plants or seeds to the Mediterranean region.

I can still buy citrons in bleak midwinter in my local market. They are a cheering and somewhat otherworldly presence in the darker months; large, elongated and grotesquely beautiful, with an intensely alive aroma and acutely puckered and pock-marked skin. Considering a citron is like coming face-to-face with the dark and mysterious past of a modern-day lemon, an almost prehistoric relic, the lemon that time forgot, a lemon as it was before humans began meddling, like some kind of monstrous pre-Darwin-discovery Galapagos lizard. Engorged and three times the size of a modern lemon, rough, bulbous and pitted, it is a prime example of something that is particularly beautiful specifically because of its asymmetrical 'ugliness'.

Unlike modern-day lemons, citrons have a thick white and foamy pith, which dominates the fruit (making up around 70 per cent of it). The pith, known as the albedo (a wonderful word) is edible, and is the prized part of the cedro in cooking, whereas the pulp is dry and bitter. The pith can be finely sliced and used in risottos and salads, and has a fragrant, very faintly-bitter flavour. It is also candied and used for panettone and traditional *dolci*.

When citron was first cultivated, like most citrus fruits, it was appreciated initially for its aroma, but in the course of history it came to have a symbolic significance too. As Alan Davidson writes in *The Oxford Companion to Food*, 'Citrus seems always to have had a curious connection with magic and religion'. Specifically, citron is known for its strong connection with Judaism; it is mentioned in the Torah as 'fruit of the most beautiful tree', perhaps even the forbidden fruit of the Garden of Eden. Known as *esrog* in Hebrew, for the ancient Jews it became the symbol of the festival of Sukkot. After their exodus from Egypt, to meet their religious requirements the Jews became travelling citron farmers, and thus became responsible for spreading the citrus, cultivating it wherever they travelled.

LEMONS IN CULTURE & COOKING

When the Arabs conquered Sicily in the 9th century, they brought their love (and ways of using) citrus with them, as well as sugar. They also introduced new irrigation techniques which allowed citrus farming to grow exponentially, enabling Sicily to become a thriving centre of citrus production. The island remained the world's most important producer until it was overtaken by California in the 20th century.

Throughout history, lemons have proved an important aesthetic inspiration, too; in the 17th century, Dutch still-life artists often used lemons in their compositions. Imported from sunnier climes, these lemons came to signify prosperity, as well as being an object of acute aesthetic beauty in themselves, often depicted whole, half-peeled or with interior segments cut open, the cut surface shining with tiny droplets. Citrus, and lemons specifically, became symbolic with wealth and exoticism; in 1533 at a banquet held for Anne Boleyn's coronation, one of the delights presented – presumably on a silver platter – was a single lemon, which had cost the princely sum of six silver pennies.

When lemons became ubiquitous in European kitchens is not entirely clear. Author Gillian Riley writes that citrus did not appear in Roman gastronomy, although some mosaics and paintings show citrus fruit. There is general consensus that lemons were known to the Arab world and, with its expansion, came to Italy. The Arabs not only used them in cooking, but believed them to have curative powers, stimulating appetite, aiding digestion and cheering a melancholy disposition.

COFFEE, LEMON & A POOR-MAN'S PUDDING

The recipes that I love the most are always told to me like secrets; whispered between fingers, mumbled through a thick moustache or shared over the top of spectacles, a finger wag or two for effect. There is a conspiratorial way that is quintessentially Italian of sharing such secrets, or *consiglie* – what we would call advice, though that's a rather cold-sounding term for it. It is often unsolicited, which can seem strange for someone unused to the habit, but if you find yourself in a shop or at a market stall, and someone tells you how to make your milk-tart wobblier, your *melanzane* sweeter, or your meatballs more tender, you know you have stumbled upon one of those moments that make every day in Italy a little bit magical.

This is not a recipe, as such, it's more a potion, which is how so many recipes began. In Massa Lubrense, a small town a little further along the Sorrentine Peninsula than Sorrento itself, I met a shopkeeper and her sister who spent an hour or so offering me such *consiglie*. Wisdom and lemon-themed knowledge poured from them like the clear, cold water that poured from the springs in the valleys surrounding us, rushing through the lemon groves and down into the town fountains to be splashed over hot heads and bathed in by bedraggled pigeons.

'Did you know,' they whispered to me in unison, leaning in and peering over pink and purple spectacles, 'that here we drink our coffee with lemon?'

I had heard such stories. They told me to peel a strip from a Sorrento lemon and place it in the top half of my moka (where the coffee collects). Then to brew my coffee as usual, but slowly, slowly, so the lemon oils have time to infuse the coffee. The next day, at a searing 6 o'clock in the morning, our balcony already white with heat and the cicadas clicking incessantly, I made a Sorrento Lemon Moka. I peeled a thick strip into the top of the pot as they had told me, and then let the coffee brew. I drank it alongside fresh ricotta and honey and toasted stone-baked Neapolitan-style bread (which is like the best pizza with dark burnished bits around the edge). The coffee with lemon was delicious: fresh and fragrant, as well as somehow both warming and cooling, and grounding and uplifting at the same time; a liquid contradiction. It will cure any headache, they had told me. Even the metaphorical ones.

The Sorrento lemon is different to its famous Amalfi cousin. It, too, is oval in shape, but generally rounder than its spindlier Sfusato neighbours and bright, canary yellow. It has a thick and fragrant pith and a slightly more acidic juice, but sweeter than lemons we know; it is still eaten whole, sometimes in salad, too. What has now become known as the Sorrento lemon is, in fact, the Femminello, which the sisters assured me originated in Massa Lubrense but has been reclaimed by the larger, more well-known town of Sorrento. In Massa, there exists one of the first cultivated lemon fields, called 'Il Gesus'; lemon cultivation having been brought and expanded in the area by the Jesuits. Lemons here were big business, they tell me, and in the old days they were like *oro* (gold), each fruit lovingly and individually packed in tissue paper to be shipped to America or England. Cultivation methods were different to those in Amalfi, too: the same chestnut-poled pergolas for supporting the trees, but a special straw matting system to cover them, to protect them from harsh weather and to delay ripening. At certain times during cultivation, the lemons would be exposed and their covering straw would then be piled up at the end of each row, in a little tepee shape; the landscape looking like some sort of elven realm, dotted with tiny straw houses and yellow dangling lemons. Now the farmers use green plastic nets, which the sisters tut at in disapproval.

The whole of this coastline (south from Naples to Maiori) is famous for lemon growing. The fruit appears everywhere, painted onto ceramic signs, stamped onto children's outfits; the shop shelves groan with lemon-printed dish towels and lemon-shaped soaps. The bars and cafés advertise the 'original lemon gelato', or sorbet, and in Amalfi fresh lemon juice is sold by the plastic cup. Outside cafés, tourists poke with pink plastic spoons at enormous semi-hollowed out lemons, piled high with snow-white sorbet, but it is not just a gimmick: the lemon here has a hallowed significance, and up until relatively recently, lemon farming was a thriving industry, now taken over by large-scale American production.

Lemon groves still dot the landscape – cut in rows into the steep cliffs are green foliage-covered frames of dark brown chestnut poles and the famous lemon terraces. Hiking the Sentiero dei Limoni, a guided path that cuts through the valley between Maiori and Minori, you weave your way among the lemon groves, though the majority of the precious fruits are hidden from view, guarded behind walls and dangling under protective canopies (the cultivation method here involves training the trees to form a protective overhead canopy, with the fruit dangling below like strings of fairy lights, so that they are sheltered from adverse weather conditions and the ripening period is extended). Interspersed with olives and vines, and marked by imagery of both lemons and donkeys (the donkey with straddling baskets for transporting lemons is an emblem of the Amalfi Coast, and you can find many a long-eared, bowed-head, ceramic specimen for sale in the shops), I followed the path at midday on a blazing Sunday in July, and met not a soul. The views of the surrounding cliffs and the endless blue sea beyond, were nothing short of spectacular. Below, little white boats left trails of powdery white spray in the water, and tiny brown bodies moved on the bustling, black volcanic beaches, punctuated with perfectly matching brightly coloured umbrellas.

Descending into Minori (home of the pale lemon-yellow Basilica di Santa Trofimena – an exact colour echo of the town's famous dessert), I stopped to eat the lemon-flavoured *dolce* of the region, the *delizia al limone*, a delightful, breast-shaped dainty of singular deliciousness. Feather-light and gratifyingly lemony, it comprises of a dome-shaped *pan di spagna*, stuffed with lemon pastry cream and soaked in a limoncello syrup, before being coated in another, lighter, white and foamy lemon-scented cream, then decorated variously with piped cream, candied lemon strips, or fresh berries. Though there are many variants the three components remain: lemon custard filling, lemon cream coating and a light *pan di spagna*. The shape, too, is always domed. Sal de Riso, the eponymous pastry shop of the famous TV pastry chef, does a famed version, which I eat alone standing at the bar. It is light, fragrant, fresh and fluffy, and I felt as though I could eat seven. De Riso also sells smells; the scents of his most beloved *dolce*, bottled, for you to spritz in your home or all over yourself, carried away on a cloud of lemon and vanilla Chantilly.

The next stop for any lemon lover is, of course, Amalfi, city of lemons and paper (two of my favourite things). The magnificent cathedral, a coloured and striped medley of mosaic, Baroque, Byzantine and Gothic styles, sits alongside another pastry must: Pansa, purveyor of candied Amalfi lemon strips and lemon-scented cream-filled croissants. Winding up the hill away from the crowds, you hear the rush of water underfoot; the streams cut through the valley were used to power the once thriving paper mills, another important industry of Amalfi. There is now only one paper mill still making paper: Amatruda, a family business who have produced *bambagina* (paper made from cloth rags) since the 15th century, but nearby you can visit the Museo della Carta and see the ancient machinery still powered by running water. Amalfi paper was once so important that it was used by the Vatican, and it was allegedly a favourite of Mozart, Byron and Oscar Wilde. Nowadays the paper is made into beautiful letter sets, luxury wedding invitations or pressed with dried flowers to sell as prints. Walking on up the valley, there are the remains of several ruined paper mills, overgrown by greenery, a vivid reminder of the once thriving industry.

The Amalfitani are fond of eating their famously fragrant lemons in slices or chunks, dressed with mint, garlic and olive oil (perhaps a little chilli or white wine vinegar, too). There is also another, simple sweet I have heard of: known as the 'poor man's pudding', or *dolci dei poveretti*, it was given to children in hard times when sweets were rare. It consists of a slice of (Amalfi) lemon sprinkled with sugar, eaten in bites like a biscuit (cookie). When I was in Amalfi I brought home some lemons and tried it for myself. It tasted like the pancakes from my childhood: so nostalgic a flavour/texture is that of tart lemon combined with the grit sweetness of sugar, that even without the pancakes themselves that was exactly what it tasted of. When I was a child, my grandma used to make us sugar sandwiches, or golden syrup sandwiches – a similarly simple hard-times treat. Sometimes, in autumn (fall), when the apples in her garden were ripe, there would be peeled apple slices in there, too. It is common among Amalfitani to offer a similar digestif of a slice of lemon sprinkled with sugar and a little ground coffee, in an echo of the Sorrentine lemon-infused moka, another combination to awaken and sharpen the senses, and further proof that coffee and lemon are a heavenly combination (see recipe, page 218).

AN ITALIAN LOVE AFFAIR

No one can deny the strong bond between Italy and citrus, and just as so many other foodstuffs we associate with Italian cooking (the tomato, for instance) were brought from elsewhere, the lemon has become a symbol and pillar of Italian – and more widely Mediterranean – cuisine.

For this reason, and based on the geography of my own Sardinian kitchen, most of the recipes that follow are Italian in their leanings, or loosely Mediterranean.

In Sardinia, almost every house has a lemon tree, and the sight of lemons drooping heavily over garden walls is as familiar as the memory of laden apples trees from my rural English childhood. Lemons grow easily here, though there has never been a real industry of lemon farming, as there was in other areas of Italy. I have planted my own lemon tree in my garden, a Quattro Stagioni, which has tiny green infant lemons hidden among baby violet leaves; their little pistils sticking out like stubby umbilical cords, they already carry an air of cheerful determination. From these tiny, sunflower-seed-sized nubs will grow beautiful lemons to use in my own kitchen at last.

A Lemon Toolkit

Lemons have become so omnipresent in the kitchen that they have their own array of gadgets made specifically to present, peel, twist and squeeze them, when lined up, look like a selection of beautifully designed, mini medieval torture weapons. Here are some of my favourites. It is important to remember that the best tool for squeezing a lemon, at least to me, is your hand, with the other hand used below like a sieve to catch the pips. However, if your hands need a rest, or you are squeezing for a large quantity, some of the items below may be of use. The precious zest, of course, requires its own tools.

A HAND-HELD LEMON SQUEEZER

is a useful (and attractive) thing to own. It is more rigorous in extracting all the juice from a lemon half than a heavy hand squeeze, and neater, too. The hand-held lemon press (not pictured) can be useful for making large quantities of lemony drinks.

A SIMPLE SWIVEL PEELER

is invaluable when using lemon zest in cooking. The flavour of a strip of lemon zest is essential in many custards and creams, particularly in the Italian kitchen. Peeling off a thick strip (with little white pith attached to it) is easy and efficient.

A GLASS LEMON SQUEEZER

is a rather beautiful object, and useful if you are squeezing a few halves for a lemony recipe. The pips often go astray and you have to squeeze only one or two at a time, pouring the juice from the spout very carefully at a gentle incline. For this reason I use mine infrequently, and only when I have a bit more time and patience.

HALF A LEMON WRAPPED IN MUSLIN

is the sort of thing you would have always been given in old-fashioned restaurants where the waiters still wore waistcoats, and is a rather stylish way of allowing people to squeeze their lemons pip-free, which always makes me think of Magritte's painting, *The Lovers*.

THE SQUIGGLE ZESTER

is a wonderful tool for making perfect little pig's-tail squiggles to decorate sweet or savoury plates. They are amazingly efficient at only removing the yellow zest rather than any white pith and have the added bonus of taking up very little space if – like me – you have a tiny kitchen.

A MICROPLANE OR FINE ZESTER

is an essential tool for any citrus zest; it is so much more precise than a box grater and takes only the very outer zest, in the finest thin strands.

A Note on Recipes

LEMONS

Lemons differ dramatically in size. The lemons I have access to here in Sardinia are always large and unwaxed, because – happily for me – they grow so well here. If the recipe calls for one (Italian) lemon, it might mean two English lemons, as imported lemons are often about half the size. When cooking the recipes make sure you always have a few lemons to spare and taste as you go along, checking for acidity and adding more juice or zest as you see fit. If you can easily get hold of Italian lemons, or Amalfi ones, then you are very lucky and should make the most of them and their leaves, too (they are often sold with their leaves still attached). If you can only buy waxed lemons, rinse them under hot water before zesting. In summer, store lemons in the refrigerator, otherwise keep them at room temperature.

SUGAR

Sugar is always regular granulated sugar. You can use granulated sugar for almost anything. I have never found any other kind of white sugar for sale here in Sardinia.

BAKING POWDER

Italian baking powder (*lievito*) is like fairy dust. It comes in brightly coloured retro packets (often aptly decorated with angels), ready-measured for a cake or batch of biscuits. One sachet is equivalent to 3 teaspoons of baking powder. It is also almost always flavoured with vanillin and so smells heavenly, adding an instant vanilla whiff to your baking. If using regular baking powder, you can opt to add a few drops of vanilla extract or simply leave it out. I find that most sweet baked goods flavoured with lemon are enhanced by a little vanilla.

OLIVE OIL & EXTRA VIRGIN OLIVE OIL

Extra virgin olive oil is the highest grade of oil, unrefined, without any additional solvents and made by cold mechanical extraction (heating and the addition of solvents changes the flavour and destroys many of the nutritional properties of the oil). I use extra virgin oil in all my sweet and savoury recipes and for frying, too, because we produce our own, and because it has a delicious, rounded, grassy flavour. However, unfortunately this oil is expensive in countries where it is not produced. In this case, I would suggest using a good extra virgin olive oil for dressings and finishing dishes, and a lower-grade one for cooking/sautéing. Your lower-grade oil should still have a mellow flavour, and should not be bitter. For deep-frying, you can use any flavourless oil of your choice.

SALT & PINCHES

I have not given precise quantities of salt, but it's important to note that 'a pinch' can vary. A scant teaspoon is about right for your cakes. Dressings and savoury dishes will need a generous pinch or two, or more. Tasting and testing is the only way you can know how much salt you like and want in your food. I always use fine sea salt.

EGGS

Eggs are all medium/large (US large/extra large), organic and free range. In baking recipes, where the size of eggs can be more important, I use medium (US large) eggs.

PECORINO

All pecorino used in the recipes is pecorino sardo rather than pecorino romano. If using pecorino romano (which is drier and saltier), add a little Parmesan, too, for rounded sweetness and depth.

Ricette

Salted Lemons

One

Lemon-marinated Olives

with Feta & Garlic

Slightly Greek its leanings, but at home all over the Mediterranean and hopefully in your kitchen too, this recipe (along with some black olives marinated with orange and fennel that an Italian friend once fed me) is the only time I think it is worth marinating olives. Choose your favourite type of olive (a kalamata or small green variety is good). Eat these as an antipasto with lots of crusty bread or focaccia.

120 ml (4 fl oz/½ cup) best-quality extra virgin olive oil
2 garlic cloves, bashed
zest of 1 lemon (peeled with a peeler) and a good squeeze of juice
1 red chilli, sliced, or a pinch of dried chilli (hot pepper) flakes
200 g (7 oz) olives
a handful of marjoram or oregano leaves (or a pinch of dried if you can't find fresh), plus extra to serve
150 g (5½ oz) feta, crumbled

Gently warm half the oil in a saucepan with the garlic until it just begins to sizzle and smell good. Add the lemon zest and chilli and cook for 1–2 minutes, then add the olives and stir through for 1–2 minutes. Add the fresh or dried herbs, reserving a little to garnish, and leave to warm for a minute to release their aroma.

Remove from the heat, and allow to cool in the pan, then mix in the lemon juice and decant the olives, lemon zest and garlic into your chosen serving dish. Top with the remaining oil and the crumbled feta, then sprinkle with some more fresh herbs and serve.

Baked Red Vegetables

with Lemon, Anchovy & Basil

A lazy summer side or vegetarian main (just add cheese and bread, or some cooked pulses and a little extra seasoning), this dish makes the most of the inherent sweetness of red peppers and tomatoes – two of the great cornerstones of summer cooking and pillars of Mediterranean cuisine. You can leave out the anchovies, if you are not a fanatic like me. The lemon zest is important here, and I like it in big strips, not finely grated.

3 large ripe red (bell) peppers
sea salt
about 120 ml (4 fl oz/½ cup)
    olive oil, plus extra for
    roasting
zest (peeled with a peeler)
    and juice of 1 lemon
300 g (10½ oz) small,
    sweet tomatoes
a pinch of dried chilli
    (hot pepper) flakes
6 anchovy fillets
a few basil leaves, torn
1 teaspoon runny honey

Preheat the oven to 150°C fan (170°C/340°F).

Halve and deseed the peppers, then cut into thick strips. Place in a roasting dish and add a few pinches of salt and a good glug of olive oil. Peel in the strips of lemon zest and throw in the tomatoes and the chilli flakes.

Roast in the oven for about 1 hour until the peppers are soft and collapsing and just browning around the edges.

Meanwhile, chop or pound the anchovies, tip into a bowl and mix in the torn basil leaves, honey, lemon juice and olive oil to make a loose dressing. Taste for seasoning and add a pinch of salt if it needs it. Toss through or drizzle over your roasted veg while they are still hot. Serve at room temperature.

Deep-fried Artichokes with Lemon Pinwheels

The artichoke, more than any other vegetable I know (except perhaps the courgette/zucchini), lends itself so willingly to deep-frying. After being steamed gently inside a crisp and salty jacket until tender and juicy, all the edible bud's myriad flavours become accentuated – the almost mushroomy nuttiness, grassy sweetness and faint background hint of lemon. This combination of crispy fried morsels makes the perfect antipasto, with added aesthetic beauty from the lemon pinwheels (which are as delicious as they are beautiful, their fleshy interiors just tinged brown on frying).

My two main go-to batter recipes for a perfectly crisp coating use either sparkling water or a beaten egg white. With artichokes, the egg white method seems to work best, as it clings to their awkward, petalled forms more persistently.

2 lemons, 1 sliced into rounds and 1 quartered
sea salt
6 globe artichokes
olive oil, for frying

FOR THE BATTER:
80 g (2¾ oz/²⁄₃ cup minus 1 tablespoon) 00 flour
110 ml (3½ fl oz/scant ½ cup) water
1 egg white

Prepare a bowl of cold water and squeeze the lemon quarters into it, then add the squeezed quarters and a big pinch of salt.

First prepare the artichokes – this stage takes the longest, although once you get the hang of it you'll find it increasingly pleasurable. Cut the stalks about 2.5 cm (1 in) from the head (if nice and tender, these are also edible). Peel away the outermost leaves and discard, then trim the base with a knife or peeler. Cut the top spiky part of the leaves away to leave a neat head and then cut in half down the centre. Using a teaspoon, scoop out the fluffy choke and discard, then cut the halves into quarters and place them in the lemon-water (this prevents them turning brown).

Now, make the batter. Place the flour in a bowl and mix in the water, whisking well to avoid any lumps. In a separate bowl whisk the egg white until just fluffy enough to hold its shape, then fold it into the batter.

Pour oil into a deep pan to a depth of about 7.5 cm (3 in) and heat to frying temperature (to test the temperature, drop a cube of bread into the oil – it should turn brown in 30 seconds).

Drain the artichoke pieces from the bowl of water and pat dry on a clean kitchen towel. Place them in the batter, a few at a time, making sure each is coated. Using a slotted spoon, carefully drop them into the hot oil. Fry for 1–2 minutes, until golden and crisp, then remove with a slotted spoon and drain on paper towels. Fry the lemon pinwheels in the same way, they will take much less time, and will brown in seconds. Drain on paper towels. Sprinkle with salt and serve.

Fried Cheese
with Lemon

Are there any two sweeter words than fried cheese? *Saganaki*, that classic Greek taverna staple, is one of my favourite things on earth, and one of the many Greek dishes that make me shiny-eyed about emigrating (I adore Greek food).

Luckily for me, the young pecorino I am able to get here in Sardinia can be treated in the same way. There are many similarities between Greek and Sardinian food – the numerous sheep's cheeses of different consistency and flavour being one example. While cheese is often roasted here in Sardinia, it is not usually fried in this way, yet the Greek technique of a hefty squeeze of lemon to cut through the fat is pure, lip-smacking heaven. As far as I am concerned, this is far superior to fried calamari rings or *fritto misto* – the textural contrast between chewy, soft and stringy cheese within and salty, fried, crunchy crust without is pure bliss.

Eat with a cold beer and, ideally, a sea view.

2 thick slabs of pecorino fresco
  (or provolone, young Gouda,
  feta or halloumi, based on
  what you have available)
a little flour
olive oil, for frying
sea salt
lemon wedges

Coat the cheese evenly in flour. Heat a good drizzle of olive oil in a heavy-based saucepan over a medium heat. Fry the cheese for a minute or two on each side until golden brown. Drain briefly on paper towels, sprinkle with salt (necessary if using a young pecorino but not with the very salty halloumi) and then serve immediately with fat wedges of lemon to squeeze over.

Burrata with Lemony Spring Vegetables

& Pistachio Pesto

Burrata is the sort of cheese you can make a meal out of, which makes it extremely useful as well as being utterly delicious. Creamy and delicate, but also rich and filling, it forms an impressive lily-white globe in the centre of a plate around which you can arrange all kinds of ingredients, all of which benefit from being doused in sweet and grassy cream once the burrata is burst into with a knife. Marinated (bell) peppers, slow-cooked courgettes (zucchini), fresh spring vegetables and roasted aubergines (eggplants) all happily form a flavoursome foundation to be crowned by a creamy ball of burrata. You can then play with various toppings and dressings. Pistachio pesto works beautifully, and in this instance enhances the verdant green of the surrounding spring vegetables, but a quick olive tapenade, fresh chilli oil or anchovy dressing would be equally delicious.

Allow half a burrata per person as a starter (appetiser) or a one per person as a main with some other salads. This is one of my favourite ways to celebrate the abundance of spring vegetables. The pesto I chop by hand as I like it chunky, but if you want to use a food processor, by all means do.

a large handful of fresh
 peas, podded
a few spears of asparagus
 (optional), chopped into
 short lengths
a large handful of fresh
 young broad (fava) beans
zest and juice of 1 large lemon
sea salt
extra virgin olive oil, for drizzling
a large handful of rocket
 (arugula)
a good handful of herbs,
 roughly chopped (I use
 mint, basil and parsley, but
 tarragon, dill, chervil and wild
 fennel would all work well)
1–2 balls of burrata

FOR THE PESTO:
60 g (2 oz) shelled pistachios
½ garlic clove, very finely chopped
sea salt
a handful of mint leaves
a handful of basil leaves
20 g (¾ oz) Parmesan or
 pecorino, finely grated
zest and juice of ½ lemon
50 ml (1²/₃ fl oz/3½ tablespoons)
 olive oil

Arrange all the fresh vegetables on a platter and scatter over the lemon zest. Squeeze over the juice, season well with salt, then drizzle over a good amount of your best oil. Mix gently, then scatter over the rocket leaves and fresh herbs.

Place the burrata in the middle of the dish, drizzle with more oil and sprinkle with some salt.

To make the pesto, roughly chop the pistachios with the garlic, salt and herbs to form a rough paste on your chopping board, then scrape into a bowl and add the grated cheese and the lemon zest. Drizzle in the olive oil and a squeeze of lemon juice until it becomes a dolloping consistency. Taste for seasoning and add more lemon or salt as required. Dollop over the burrata and salad and serve.

If you would like, serve this with some bruschetta (page 48).

Bruschetta with Stracciatella

& Anchovies, Confit Tomatoes & Lemon Zest

This is based on one of the most memorable pizza slices I have ever eaten. It was a simple pizza slice made with a good chewy and crisp dough, topped with just a hint of sweet-sharp tomato, then a large blob of creamy stracciatella and atop this a fat, juicy anchovy – so far, so familiar – but the final flourish adorning the fishy sliver was a tiny and perfect squiggle of lemon zest. This fragrant touch was utterly inspired and altered the entire dish, elevating it into something completely different and delicious.

Stracciatella is the exploded inside of a burrata (strings of mozzarella muddled with cream). If you can't find it, smush a burrata onto the bruschetta for much the same result.

If you are a keen pizza maker, by all means make your signature dough and top it with this (lemon squiggle, straciatella and anchovy *after* cooking), otherwise you can cut a wee corner and make the most wonderful bruschetta of your life. As with all 'things on toast', the quality of the ingredients is key. This is equally true of pizza.

4 slices of your best bread
  (I like a white sourdough)
best-quality extra virgin
  olive oil
sea salt
a few tomatoes or a couple
  of fresh sweet ones
4 generous tablespoons
  stracciatella (or burrata)
4 fat anchovy fillets
4 little squiggles of lemon zest

Preheat the oven to 160°C fan (180°C/350°F).

Put the bread onto a baking tray (pan), drizzle with olive oil and sprinkle with a pinch of salt, then toast in the preheated oven for 10–15 minutes. Alternatively, griddle the bread until toasted.

You can either use the fresh sweet tomatoes as they are, or confit them. To confit the tomatoes, throw them into a baking tray with a drizzle of olive oil and a sprinkle of salt in the preheated oven and roast for 10–15 minutes as long as your bread cooks, until they burnish and burst.

Top each slice of bread with a couple of squished confit tomatoes, a generous dollop of stracciatella and then a fat anchovy. Finish with a little curl of lemon zest, then drizzle with lots of extra oil and eat with your fingers, messily.

Pizzette with Lemon, Sausage & Fennel

MAKES 4
PIZZETTE

A miniature pizza (the coquettishly named *pizzetta*) provides a perfect opportunity to trial numerous flavour combinations. Here, salty aged pecorino and savoury sausage are lifted by lemon and the ethereal aniseedy flavour of fennel, adapted from a happy sausage and lemon combination I discovered via food writer Catherine Phipps. Pork and lemon are familiar bedfellows, so it makes sense that sausage and lemon combine harmoniously, too. I have Sardinia-fied it by adding aged pecorino and fresh fennel, both of which have lemony notes of their own.

I love *pizzette* – they're more frivolous and forgiving than feeling that you must toil to produce a perfect, Neapolitan-style, photo-worthy, full-sized pizza. They look instantly pretty in all their irregular oval charm, allow you to be creative with toppings and have an instantly celebratory feel, even if it's just you and your family (perhaps you and yourself, even) eating them at home on a Friday night (which it very often is). Once you have made your dough, the rest is easy.

I use semola (finely milled durum wheat) in all of my doughs, as it makes them extra spongey and flavourful, but if you can't find it use all bread flour. One thing I cannot live without since moving to Italy is the drizzle of extra virgin olive oil that crowns the pizza fresh out of the oven. It's essential and elevates all the existing flavours.

FOR THE DOUGH:
100 g (3½ oz/⅔ cup) semola
150 g (5½ oz/1 cup) strong
  white bread flour
160 ml (5½ fl oz/⅔ cup)
  warmish water
7 g (¼ oz) fresh yeast
  (or 4 g/⅛ oz dried yeast)
5 g (1 teaspoon) sea salt

FOR THE TOPPINGS:
about 2 Italian sausages, cut
  into chunks, or 150 g (5½ oz)
  sausage meat
1 small fennel bulb, thinly sliced
3 balls of mozzarella, drained
  and cut/torn into pieces
50 g (1¾ oz) aged pecorino, grated
1 lemon, zested, then cut into a few
  very thin slices and quartered

TO SERVE:
basil leaves
dried chilli (hot pepper)
  flakes (optional)
extra virgin olive oil

Make your dough by mixing all of the ingredients together (either by hand or in a mixer), then kneading until you have a smooth and elastic dough.

Place the dough back in the bowl and cover with a plastic bag. Leave to rise in a warm place for about an hour, ideally until doubled in size.

Preheat the oven to the highest temperature (you can also preheat your baking tray (pan) or pizza stone if you're a pizza pro).

Once risen, divide the dough into four pieces, roll them out into rough ovals and place on baking parchment. Top with small chunks of sausage, a couple of slices of fennel, some mozzarella pieces and some grated pecorino. Scatter over a little lemon zest and a thin quarter-slice of lemon or two.

Bake in a very hot oven for about 10 minutes until golden. Serve with fresh basil leaves, chilli flakes and a drizzle of your best olive oil.

Note: It is important to cut and drain the mozzarella before topping your pizza, otherwise it tends to make the dough soggy.

Lemon
IN
SALADS

& Lemons on Greens

There are few vegetables, whether raw or cooked, that are not improved by a little fresh lemon juice or zest. When dressing salads, I almost always use fresh lemon juice as my base acidity (for more on this) – and, more often than not, I use their freshly grated zest too.

When I worked for Skye Gyngell at Spring, one of the most important things I learnt was the art of making vegetables delicious. On the salad section, we always had a huge pot of fresh lemon halves for freshly squeezed juice, and then a pot of freshly grated lemon zest as well. This lemon zest we sprinkled through almost every salad and plenty of cooked vegetables, too, as it contributes its characteristic fragrant lift. Next to the pot of zest was a pot of finely grated Parmesan, which was often used to balance it. The sweet, savoury, nutty depth of the cheese offsets the acidity of the lemon, and the two ingredients (when mixed with lemon juice, good olive oil and salt) make a perfectly harmonious dressing for all number of things (we used it for cooked beetroot (beets), raw fennel, cooked spinach, rocket (arugula) leaves, watercress, cooked broccoli, turnips, radishes…the list is endless).

The inherent sweetness of both raw and cooked vegetables works beautifully when piqued by a little fresh lemon juice and a fragrant hint of zest. Root vegetables, aubergines (eggplants) and (bell) peppers (once cooked, especially roasted) are perhaps more obvious contenders for a spritz of fresh juice or sprinkle of zest, as they are so blatantly sweet, but one of my favourite uses for lemon, which is perhaps slightly less obvious, is with cooked greens.

In Italy it is common to cook greens and then allow them to cool before dressing them with olive oil, salt, and perhaps a little lemon, then eating them either cold or at room temperature. Cooked spinach, broccoli, turnip tops, dandelion and chicories are absolutely delicious eaten in this way. Their iron-rich and inherently green flavour is best appreciated when eaten cool, and accentuated with a little lemon juice (and/or zest). Similarly, in Greece, one of my favourite traditional dishes is *horta*, a plate of wilted wild greens (mostly slightly bitter) dressed in olive oil and served with a giant wedge of fresh lemon on the side, for squeezing liberally over. The same treatment works incredibly well with all manner of vegetables. Simply cook them in salted water until tender, then drain, refresh briefly in cold water, dress with your best olive oil and serve with a spritz of lemon juice and/or a sprinkle of zest. Add a little extra sea salt if you like. I particularly recommend bitter greens, but it is also excellent with peas, green beans, flat beans, beetroot and cauliflower.

Shaved Fennel & Lemon Salad

Although I hesitate to use the word 'clean' when describing food, there really is no other term that captures the fresh purity of this salad. It is a combination of tumbling pale green and yellow citrussy shards that Mauro, my father-in-law, often makes, and which provides the perfect foil to rich roasted chicken or pork, though it is also a lovely thing in its own right.

This is the simplest and most basic version of the salad, but you can use it as a building block for many other delicious additions, like shards of cheese (feta, ricotta salata, pecorino), herbs, nuts, seeds, anchovies, olives, etc. If you are able to buy citrons – a variety of citrus with a thicker, edible pith – they work beautifully in this recipe.

4 large fennel bulbs
2 lemons
sea salt
extra virgin olive oil

Top and tail the fennel bulbs and cut it in half lengthways. Reserve the fronds and remove any large, woody outer pieces. Shave or thinly slice into a bowl. Squeeze the juice of one lemon over the fennel and then add a good few pinches of salt and a very generous glug of good olive oil. Toss well until everything is slick and coated.

Cut the remaining the lemon into quarters and discard any pips, then cut into thin slices and toss through the salad. Season again to taste and serve drizzled with some extra oil and scattered with the fennel fronds.

Lemony Courgette Scapece

The combination of lemons and courgettes (zucchini) pops up in numerous instances in this book. It is no coincidence as they are a wonderful match and the perfect example of the lemon as an enhancer and facilitator, an ingredient that can coax out the best in another. A raw courgette's nutty, vegetal, almost almond-like sweetness is accentuated when sharply dressed with lemon and tossed in a salad (add some shavings of Parmesan or ricotta salata), while a cooked courgette's silky sweetness is perfectly balanced by a squeeze of juice.

In this recipe the courgettes are cooked in a sort of *scapece*, or what you may know as *escabeche*. *Scapece* is an inheritance from the Spanish domination of southern Italy and is particularly common in Naples, where it is usually made with courgettes. It comes from the Spanish word for what in Italian is called *inzuppare*, which translates literally to 'in soup'. A wonderful expression. Here, the courgettes are fried and then doused in a minty-lemony-garlic mixture, then left to marinate before being served at room temperature. They make a very welcome addition to a barbecue or light lunch of cheese, bread and salad. If you have baby courgettes, like those pictured, you can halve them lengthways and griddle them whole.

500 g (1 lb 2 oz) courgettes (zucchini), thinly sliced
sea salt
2–3 sprigs of mint, leaves chopped
1 large garlic clove, thinly sliced
30 ml (2 tablespoons) extra virgin olive oil, plus extra for frying
juice of ½ large lemon and a little zest

Heat a few tablespoons of oil in a shallow frying pan (skillet) over a high heat. Quickly fry the courgette discs in batches (don't overcrowd the pan otherwise they don't colour nicely), turning once. Make sure they do not become too dark or remain too pale – they should take on a nice caramel colour at the edges. Drain and dab on paper towels once cooked, then sprinkle them with sea salt.

Mix the mint and garlic with the oil and lemon juice and zest in a bowl to make a dressing. Add a pinch of salt and taste.

Place the drained and salted courgettes in a bowl and douse them in the dressing. Stir to distribute and leave for at least an hour before eating (in theory! They'll be good straight away, but get better with time). Eat at room temperature.

Double Bean Salad

The final touches to almost any dish based around pulses should be a little lemon and a drizzle of good olive oil. The intensely sweet, earthy beaniness benefits from both a lemony lift and the punch of a good green oil. Equally, cooked chickpeas (garbanzos) and lentils are infinitely improved by these essential additions.

In this salad, which is a favourite for outside lunches in the summer, white beans are served at room temperature with pan-fried green beans, dressed in a sharp lemony dressing and topped with soft-boiled eggs, capers and a lemon and dill vinaigrette. Ripe sliced beef tomatoes would be a welcome addition, as would anchovies, boiled potatoes, tuna, olives (for a lemony Niçoise-style salad). This also makes a lovely summer side dish to serve with roasted or barbecued chicken.

2 tablespoons extra virgin olive oil, plus extra for drizzling
1 garlic clove, bashed
250 g (9 oz) green beans, topped and tailed
a handful of sweet tomatoes (datterini or cherry)
sea salt
zest and juice of 1 lemon
250 g (9 oz) cooked cannellini or butter (lima) beans (from a jar, tin or carton), rinsed under cold running water (drained weight)
a handful of rocket (arugula), watercress or young spinach
a handful each of parsley and dill (basil is also nice), leaves chopped, plus extra to serve
2 eggs
a handful of capers
crusty bread, to serve

FOR THE VINAIGRETTE:
1 teaspoon Dijon mustard
1 teaspoon runny honey
juice of ½ lemon
80 ml (5 tablespoons) extra virgin olive oil
1 scant teaspoon sea salt

Heat the olive oil in a frying pan (skillet) with the garlic over a medium heat, then add the green beans and tomatoes. Cook tossing occasionally, until the beans take on a little colour and the tomatoes burst. Remove the garlic clove and discard. Add a splash or two of water if things get too hot. Once the beans are just tender and squeaky, season them well with salt, olive oil and some lemon zest and juice and remove from the heat.

Toss the white beans in salt, oil and lemon juice until they are flavoursome, then lay them on a platter with the green leaves and herbs scattered around. Scatter over the green beans and tomatoes.

Place the eggs in a saucepan of water, bring the water to a rolling boil and cook for 6 minutes, then peel the eggs under cold running water. Cut the eggs in half and place them on top of the salad.

To make the vinaigrette, quickly mix all the ingredients together in a bowl, then drizzle over the top. Serve with some extra scattered herbs, the capers and good crusty bread for mopping up juices. You will have a good amount of vinaigrette left for other occasions (store it in the refrigerator).

Cabbage & Kohlrabi Salad

with Whole Lemon, Pecorino, Chilli & Pine Nuts

One of the great travesties in vegetable cookery is the overcooking of any member of the brassica family. The versatile and various members of this family (which include broccoli, kohlrabi, cauliflower and turnips) are all descended from the same wild cabbage (*Brassica oleracea*) and all have similar flavour profiles. When eaten raw or cooked correctly they are sweet and nutty, with just the faintest background note of pleasing bitterness, but when overboiled they can become sulphurous and unpleasantly bitter. This bitterness and eggy taste also increase over time, so when cooking or serving them in salads, make sure they are as fresh as possible. There is a great difference between a just-picked brassica and a four-day-old, yellowing-leaved version.

One of my favourite ways to eat any brassica is raw. Brussels sprouts make a sensational salad when finely sliced, mixed with shards of pecorino and plenty of lemon and olive oil, as does any good, fresh, crisp cabbage. Kohlrabi – that odd, alien-like vegetable known in Italy as *cavolo rapa* – is the sweetest brassica of them all; when fresh and young it almost tastes like a green apple. I love to use it in salads (sometimes with green apples, too, for a double fresh and apple-y hit) and it works so well when seasoned liberally with lemon to counteract its sweetness. It needs to be peeled of the tough outer skin and have its stubby stems removed (these can be used to flavour soups, etc).

This is one of the salads where I like to add whole pieces of lemon. It's not a precise recipe, as it's more of an assembly job. Serve as a side to a lemony roast chicken, some grilled pork chops or alongside the lemon and fennel bake (page 70).

Other welcome additions are some watercress or other peppery green leaves, and sliced raw fennel. Any cabbage family member works brilliantly in this way (try Brussels sprouts too). Switch the olive oil for sesame oil for a change, with some fresh sesame seeds too.

30 g (1 oz/2 tablespoons) pine
nuts (or sesame seeds)
1 sweetheart cabbage (savoy
or white cabbage also work),
halved, cored and finely
shredded
a large handful of rocket
(arugula), young spinach
and/or watercress leaves
2 kohlrabi, peeled, halved and
thinly sliced (use a mandoline
if you have one)
a handful of herbs, roughly
chopped (mint, parsley and
dill work well, I like a mix
of all three)
sea salt
4 tablespoons finely grated
Parmesan or pecorino (or
feta), plus shavings to serve
a pinch of dried chilli (hot
pepper) flakes
120 ml (4 fl oz/½ cup) extra
virgin olive oil
1 small firm lemon, or ½ large
lemon
½ teaspoon runny honey

Toast the pine nuts in a frying pan (skillet) over a very low heat
for 1–2 minutes, tossing occasionally, until pale golden. Set
aside. If using sesame seeds, toast them in a similar way.

Mix the shredded cabbage with the leaves, sliced kohlrabi and
herbs in a bowl. Add the Parmesan, chilli flakes and olive oil,
season with salt and toss until everything is coated.

Quarter the lemon and remove any pips. Halve each quarter
and then finely slice them lengthways to make mini thin
wedges. Toss into the salad and stir again with your hands.

Mix the honey with a squeeze of lemon juice to dissolve it,
pour over the salad and toss again. Taste for seasoning and add
more chilli/salt/lemon juice/olive oil as you see fit. It should be
punchy and sharp.

Serve sprinkled with the toasted pine nuts and some shavings
of Parmesan or pecorino.

Lemony Minestra

A tub of ready-to-go cannellini beans is invaluable when you are short of time or what the Italians call *voglia* (which translates as 'want' or 'desire'). Of course there are always tins, jars and cartons if you don't have time to soak and cook them yourself, but if you have been fruitful and cooked them, they can sit in the refrigerator for a good few days and wait to be used. The added bonus of cooking them yourself is that you can flavour them with anything you wish (perhaps some onion or garlic; herbs such as bay, thyme, rosemary or sage; a sun-dried tomato or two; or any combination of these), and they make a great starting point for this broth.

I cooked these simply with water, a few tablespoons of oil, a clove or two of garlic and a sprig of rosemary, which meant they were the perfect bland carbohydrate-canvas to build on, and allowed the simple sweet and summery flavours of the other ingredients to stand out. You can use a stock cube or homemade stock as you wish.

1 red onion, sliced
1 small celery stalk, diced
1 garlic clove, sliced
4 tablespoons olive oil
2 small courgettes (zucchini), halved lengthways and sliced into crescents
150 g (5½ oz/1 cup) cooked cannellini beans with their juice
400 ml (14 fl oz/generous 1½ cups) stock (vegetable or chicken is fine)
100 g (3½ oz) small frozen peas
sea salt
a handful of parsley, roughly chopped
zest and juice of 1 small lemon
15 g (½ oz/3 tablespoons) Parmesan or pecorino, grated
extra virgin olive oil, to serve
dried chilli (hot pepper) flakes (optional), to serve

In a large saucepan, sauté the onion, celery and garlic in the oil over a medium-low heat until beginning to soften and turn golden (around 10 minutes at least). Add the sliced courgettes and sauté, stirring occasionally, until the vegetables become golden and begin to caramelise (add a splash or two of water if necessary).

Once the courgettes are collapsing and caramelised, add the cannellini beans, stock and peas and allow to bubble for at least 5 minutes until the broth has thickened and gained a little flavour. Taste for seasoning and add salt if necessary. Cook, covered, until al dente (you may need to add a little more water at this point if necessary).

Add the chopped parsley, lemon zest and juice, grated cheese and a good glug of extra virgin olive oil. Scatter over the chilli flakes, if using.

Feta, Lemon & Melon Salad

SERVES 2 AS A
MAIN OR 4 AS
A STARTER/
SIDE SALAD

All members of the same family (the vast *Cucurbitaceae*), these high-summer vegetables make happy bedfellows on the plate. Cucumbers come from the same genus as melons (gourds), and the two are often paired in salads or cold soups, whereas courgettes (zucchini) hail from a different family branch (along with squash) and make a welcome addition. Sweet, juicy and nutty on the palate, the vegetables are offset by plenty of lemon dressing and some toasty pumpkin seeds (pepitas) and salty feta. A perfect summer medley. I like to finish with lemon squiggles (a technical term!) for both aesthetics and a proper hit of zesty flavour. The salad leaves are optional, but I like the green and all salads to me need a little leaf.

50 g (1¾ oz/⅓ cup) pumpkin
  seeds (pepitas)
1 small ripe melon (cantaloupe
  is good, as is a large wedge
  of watermelon)
2 cucumbers
2 courgettes (zucchini)
juice of 1 lemon
a handful of lamb's lettuce or
  rocket (arugula) (optional)
a few sprigs of mint, leaves
  chopped
1 block of feta (or roughly
  80 g/2¾ oz goat's cheese)
sea salt
extra virgin olive oil
lemon zest squiggles, to serve

Toast the pumpkin seeds in a dry frying pan (skillet) over a low heat for a few minutes until they pop and brown slightly.

Skin the melon, deseed and cut into slices. Peel the cucumbers and cut into thick discs, along with the courgettes.

Place the vegetables and salad leaves, if using, in a bowl and toss with plenty of lemon juice and olive oil and a few pinches of salt. Taste and adjust the seasoning.

Stir the mint through the salad leaves, then place on a platter or in a serving bowl and scatter over the pumpkin seeds. Crumble over the feta, add another drizzle of oil and the lemon squiggles and serve.

Spring Fregola Salad

SERVES 4
AS A SIDE

Fregola is a Sardinian pasta made by rolling grains of semolina together to form small balls and then toasting them in an oven. The finished pasta has a toasty, smoky flavour, a wonderful nubbly texture and is just small/large enough to provide a nutty chew (and occasionally get caught in a windpipe as you greedily inhale large mouthfuls). It is incredibly versatile and delicious, and can be cooked like rice or pasta; here it is boiled like pasta and then allowed to cool before becoming the basis of a substantial salad. The smokiness works well with the sweetness of young raw courgettes (zucchini), and some toasted almonds top everything off perfectly. A good side dish with roast fish or white meats, or a nice summer salad on its own.

250 g (9 oz) fregola
150 g (5½ oz) frozen peas
sea salt
50–60 ml (1¾–2 fl oz/ 3½–4 tablespoons) extra virgin olive oil, plus extra to serve
zest and juice of 1 lemon
3 small courgettes (zucchini), sliced or peeled into strips
a handful of sweet herbs (mint, parsley, dill leaves), roughly chopped, plus extra to serve
40 g (1½ oz/⅓ cup) flaked (slivered) almonds, toasted
150 g (5½ oz) fresh ricotta

Cook the fregola in a large saucepan of boiling salted water until al dente, adding the frozen peas to the pan a minute before the fregola is done. Drain and rinse quickly under cold running water. Drain again and place in a bowl, allowing the fregola to cool and stirring occasionally to prevent it sticking.

When the fregola has cooled, season it well with salt, plentiful olive oil and lemon juice and zest. Taste for seasoning and adjust accordingly (the fregola will drink oil!).

Toss the courgette ribbons through the fregola and then add a little more seasoning if necessary. Toss through the herbs, reserving a few to garnish.

Arrange on a serving platter and top with large blobs of ricotta, sprinkle over some extra herbs and the almonds, and drizzle with a little extra oil to finish.

Creamy Fennel, Lemon & Pecorino Bake

SERVES 4–6

At one of my favourite restaurants of all time – The Seahorse in Dartmouth, Devon – a small silver dish of sliced fennel baked in cream is served alongside baked white fish. The fennel is pale, delicate, sweet and savoury and provides the perfect accompaniment. It looks beautiful too, in all of its elven pale green-white splendour.

This is a gilded version of the same thing, lifted by a double hit of lemon and given a savoury punch by garlic and anchovies. If you prefer to keep it vegetarian, leave out the anchovies and it will still be delicious. It can be a meal in itself (with a sharp, lemon-dressed green salad) or a side dish for pork, chicken or fish. The lemon cuts through the cream perfectly and stops it being too rich.

butter, for greasing
2 large or 3 small fennel bulbs
300 ml (10 fl oz/1¼ cups) double (heavy) cream
50 ml (1¾ fl oz/ 3½ tablespoons) milk
1 lemon, zested and quartered
sea salt
1 garlic clove, bashed
80 g (2¾ oz/1 cup) grated pecorino
30 g (1 oz/½ cup) coarse breadcrumbs, preferably chunky and from a rustic loaf (dried breadcrumbs also work)
extra virgin olive oil, for drizzling
6 anchovy fillets

Preheat the oven to 170°C fan (190°C/375°F). Grease a gratin dish with butter.

Trim the roots and stems from the fennel, chop and reserve the fronds and slice the fennel lengthways into thinnish slices, about 3–4 mm (⅛ in) thick.

Bring a pan of well-salted water to the boil and cook the fennel for 3 minutes until just tender. Drain and arrange in the gratin dish.

In a saucepan, heat the cream and milk with half the lemon zest, a pinch of salt, the chopped fennel fronds and the garlic clove. When coming to the boil, remove the pan from the heat and add half the pecorino. Stir to dissolve.

Chop a quarter of the lemon into thin slices, then chop these slices into little pieces and scatter over the fennel. Pour over the cream mixture, removing the bashed garlic clove as you do so.

Mix the remaining lemon zest with the breadcrumbs and remaining cheese for the topping. Sprinkle this over the fennel and cream and drizzle with the olive oil. Dot over the anchovy fillets, if using.

Bake in the oven for about 40 minutes until golden and bubbling.

Saffron Tagliatelle

with Fresh Tomato & Lemon

This is a zingier, fresher take on the beloved and classic *pasta al sugo*. It's important to use the sweetest tomatoes (datterini) to counteract the sharpness of the lemon. A few anchovies melted in at the beginning are also very welcome, if you're an anchovy addict like me. Olives are a good addition, as are capers, parsley, tuna, rocket (arugula)... I could go on. Otherwise, keep it simple and relish the sweet-sour of those classic cornerstones of Mediterranean cookery: lemon and tomato.

Making your own tagliatelle is easy and satisfying, and allows you to flavour and colour it with saffron, but if you're short on time add a pinch of saffron to the sauce and use ready-made tagliatelle. Grating an onion provokes stinging tears, but it is quick and effective at extracting all of its sweetness once gently sautéed in olive oil. I grate it directly into the pan with the oil.

FOR THE TAGLIATELLE:
2 eggs
200 g (7 oz/1⅓ cups) semola
  or 00 flour, plus extra
  for dusting
½ teaspoon ground saffron

FOR THE SAUCE:
2 tablespoons best-quality
  extra virgin olive oil
½ small white onion
200 g (7 oz) Datterini tomatoes
1 lemon, a few strips of peeled
  zest and a squeeze of juice
a good pinch of sea salt
1 teaspoon sugar or light
  honey
marjoram, basil or
  parsley leaves, to serve

First, make the pasta. Using either a stand mixer with a dough hook or your hands, mix the eggs into the semola, then add the saffron and then knead it into the dough until smooth. Leave to rest wrapped in cling film (plastic wrap) for about 20 minutes.

Roll out the dough until just thin enough to see through (about the thickness of a penny). Cut into 1 cm (½ in) wide strips by hand or using your pasta machine and set aside, well dusted with extra semola to stop it sticking.

To make the sauce, heat the oil in a deep frying pan (skillet) over a low heat and grate the onion into it. Sauté until soft and translucent. Halve the tomatoes, throw them in and turn the heat up (it will spit and hiss a bit, but not to worry). Cook until the tomatoes begin to collapse, then add the strips of lemon zest and continue cooking for a few minutes. Add the salt, sugar or honey and taste for seasoning. Add a squeeze of the lemon juice.

Cook the pasta in a large saucepan of well-salted boiling water until al dente. Drain the pasta and stir through the sauce, adjust the seasoning and serve with plenty of marjoram, basil or parsley scattered over, an extra drizzle of oil and a grating of fresh lemon zest.

Lemon & Courgette Carbonara

When I talk about a dish as a 'carbonara', I mean the method of creating a creamy pasta sauce with eggs that are cooked just enough to emulsify and thicken but not so much as to become scrambled or solid. I prefer carbonara sauces made without the traditional pancetta/guanciale, as I find the classic version of the dish quite heavy, so I instead like to use vegetables. Artichokes, peas, broad (fava) beans and braised greens all make delicious carbonaras, as do courgettes (zucchini).

This courgette carbonara is lifted by a hefty hit of lemon (both zest and juice), which cuts through the richness of the eggs beautifully. It is also essential to counteract the sweetness of the braised courgettes, which become almost jammy after slow sautéing in plentiful olive oil and garlic. Courgette and lemon is a combination you will often see in my recipes, and it is a happy and mutually complementary marriage; the sweetness of the vegetable is cut by the acidity of the fruit, and the innate lemony-ness of courgettes accentuated by both the zest and juice of the citrus.

Choose small, young courgettes if you can find them, their flavour is superior and they have a lower water content. I also use pecorino sardo, which has both a lemony flavour and nutty sweetness that work perfectly here. If you can't find it, use Parmesan or a mix of pecorino romano and Parmesan.

I often make the sautéed courgettes the night before, and keep them in the refrigerator before putting this together the next day for a last-minute lunch. I like using smooth penne, but spaghetti or rigatoni also work well.

4 tablespoons extra virgin olive oil, plus extra to serve
1 garlic clove, bashed
2 medium or 3 small courgettes (zucchini), sliced in half lengthways, then into half-moons
sea salt
180 g (6½ oz) pasta of your choice
1 egg plus 2 egg yolks
4 tablespoons grated pecorino (or Parmesan)
zest of 1 small lemon and juice of ½
basil leaves, to serve

Heat the oil in a frying pan (skillet) over a medium-low heat, then fry the garlic clove until it just begins to sizzle and smell good. Add the courgette slices and sauté, stirring regularly, until they are golden all over, beginning to break down and almost jammy. Season well with salt and set aside (or leave to cool, then keep in the refrigerator for future use).

Cook the pasta according to the packet instructions in a large pan of well-salted boiling water until al dente.

Meanwhile, mix the egg and egg yolks, cheese and lemon into the courgette mixture, and begin to heat very gently, stirring all the time. Scoop out the pasta with a slotted spoon straight into the courgette pan along with a splash or two of the cooking water. Stir and toss over a low heat until you have a creamy sauce that coats the pasta. Taste for seasoning, add a few fresh basil leaves, extra Parmesan and a drizzle of your best oil, then serve.

Variation: Artichoke Carbonara

Make as opposite for courgette carbonara, but in place of the courgettes, use 4–5 prepared, sliced artichoke hearts (page 42), and finish with chopped mint rather than basil.

Creamy Lemon Linguine

A simplified version of one of my most frequently made recipes, which in turn was based on a most beloved Nigella Lawson recipe. The original recipe uses double (heavy) cream, but I use mascarpone as it is easier to get hold of in Italy and works perfectly here. I have never met a creamy lemon pasta dish that I didn't like.

200 g (7 oz) linguine
2 egg yolks
100 g (3½ oz/½ cup)
  mascarpone
2 tablespoons grated pecorino
zest of 1 lemon and juice of ½
30 g (1 oz/2 tablespoons) butter
sea salt
a few basil leaves, torn
extra virgin olive oil, to serve

Cook the pasta in a large saucepan of well-salted boiling water until al dente. Drain the pasta, reserving a little of the cooking water just in case the sauce needs it (although I rarely need it here). Return the pasta to the pan.

Meanwhile, mix together the egg yolks, mascarpone, pecorino and lemon zest and juice in a bowl. Add a pinch of salt and the butter and set aside.

Throw the sauce into the pan of drained pasta and stir vigorously, over the lowest heat, tossing the linguine well until every strand is coated and saucy. Taste for seasoning, adding more salt or lemon juice if you see fit. Add the torn basil leaves, stir quickly and serve, with a drizzle of extra virgin olive oil if you like.

Spaghetti with Tuna & Lemons

This is a combination of lots of different recipes all thrown into one, a sort of improved AOP (*spaghetti aglio olio e peperoncino* – the simplest classic Italian pasta dish of fried garlic olive oil and chilli) and a happy mess of things that are often found at the back of the refrigerator or cupboard. It's a lovely light winter lunch, to blast away the cobwebs and keep things sharp and fresh with the tang of capers, a lift of lemon zest and the peppery punch of rocket (arugula). If available, I like to use spaghettoni – a slightly plumper spaghetti, with fatter, more robust strands – but any long pasta shape would be good.

The 'sauce' – though this is less of a sauce and more of a saucy 'coating' – is the work of seconds, and is wonderfully savoury and satisfying. Another reason to love tinned (or more often, jarred) tuna.

As he eats his plateful, my husband Lorenzo carefully picks out every individual caper and leaves them in a neat pile on the side of his plate, but he says he wouldn't like it as much if they weren't there. That's the funny thing about capers: even if you don't like them, you can still appreciate them for all their salty oddness. (He says he appreciates them in all their caper-bility but would rather not eat a whole one. He is obviously thrilled with this pun.)

200 g (7 oz) spaghetti
4 tablespoons olive oil,
  plus extra to serve
2 garlic cloves, thinly sliced
a small glass white wine
1 x 150 g (5½ oz) tin of tuna
  in oil, drained
zest of 1 small lemon
a pinch of dried chilli (hot
  pepper) flakes
a large handful of rocket
  (arugula), large leaves
  roughly chopped, small
  leaves left whole
a little chopped parsley
  (optional)
1 scant tablespoon capers
sea salt

Cook the pasta according to the packet instructions in a large saucepan of well-salted boiling water until al dente.

Meanwhile, heat the oil in a large saucepan, add the garlic to sauté it until just turning golden. Pour in the glass of wine and allow to boil for a minute or two, then add the tuna and stir for a minute. Add the lemon zest, chilli flakes, rocket and parsley, if using. Finally, add the capers and taste for seasoning. Add a pinch of salt and a spritz of lemon if necessary, or a bit more chilli for heat. Set aside.

Drain the pasta, reserving a few tablespoons of the cooking water. Add both pasta and cooking water to the tuna pan over a medium heat and place over the heat again for a couple of minutes. Toss and stir to make sure the pasta is well coated. Check the seasoning again and serve with an extra drizzle of olive oil.

Prawn, Chilli & Lemon Zest Linguine

SERVES 2

It was Luca, my ex-boyfriend and the person who introduced me to Sardinia, who taught me how to cook and prepare prawn (shrimp) spaghetti properly. He loved prawns so much it became his nickname, especially as his particular pronunciation of the word itself was so wonderful, the 'w' becoming a sort of 'u', making it rhyme with brown rather than brawn.

He loved cooking prawns, he loved peeling them, he loved eating them. He belligerently barbecued prawns in the park, he lovingly beheaded prawns in our tiny galley kitchen, he crunched fried prawns in restaurants and sucked their pink prawn heads dry. He taught me that to make any good dish based on prawns (except perhaps prawn cocktail – but that's another story) you have to buy them raw and whole, and that the heads and shells are where the gold lies. To make the best prawn spaghetti of all, you need to make a quick stock out of the heads and shells (the word stock immediately inspires fear and reluctance, but this is literally the work of minutes) and use this as the sauce for your pasta. This pale pink nectar is so rich, deep and sweet, it begs for a lift of lemon zest and a squeeze of juice, which, rounded off with fresh parsley and a little kick of chilli, makes one of the most paradisiacal plates any prawn could wish for.

I only buy fresh prawns about twice a year, but when I do, this is how I want to eat them, raising a glass to Luca as I do.

500 g (1 lb 2 oz) raw prawns (shrimp) in their shells, heads on
4–5 tablespoons extra virgin olive oil, plus extra to serve
2 garlic cloves, bashed
2 small glasses dry white wine
200 g (7 oz) linguine
a pinch of dried chilli (hot pepper) flakes
a handful of small sweet tomatoes, chopped/halved (optional)
a handful of chopped parsley leaves
zest and juice of ½ lemon
sea salt

First, prepare the prawns. Off with their heads! Set the heads aside on a plate along with the shells. Remove and discard the tails from the prawns. Cut a little slit down the backs of the prawns and remove the black vein (if you're not squeamish you can skip this step and eat the whole prawn).

To make the stock, pour 1–2 tablespoons of the olive oil into a small saucepan set over a medium-low heat. Add one of the garlic cloves to the pan. Throw in the prawn shells and heads and roast for a few minutes, stirring occasionally. Once they are all pink and slightly roasty, add the wine and allow to simmer as your pasta water comes to the boil.

Cook the pasta in a large saucepan of well-salted boiling water until al dente.

Meanwhile, heat the remaining olive oil with the remaining garlic clove and the chilli flakes in a sauté pan over a medium heat. Add the prawns and fry for a minute or two on each side, then add the tomatoes, cook for a minute, then set aside.

Once the pasta is al dente, drain it and add it the pan
with the prawns along with the strained prawn stock. Toss
over the heat for a minute or two until it all comes together,
then add the chopped parsley, lemon zest and juice. Taste
for seasoning, adding salt and more lemon if necessary,
add another drizzle of oil and serve.

Lemon, Almond & Mint Pesto Pasta

A punchy pesto that prickles with lemon zest and juice and sings with the sparkling freshness of mint. The fragrant zest cuts through the garlic, cheese and nuts and makes this somehow much cleaner tasting, in the most delightful way (to borrow the words of Mary Poppins).

I use almonds (more versatile and less expensive than the pine nuts traditionally used in pesto) and roast them a little (the toastiness works well to balance the zing of the lemon). As the herbal element, I like a mixture of fresh-tasting mint and parsley. The cheesy component is a mix of pecorino and Parmesan, but if you can't find pecorino, use all Parmesan. I have come to prefer this to the classic pesto.

40 g (1½ oz) blanched almonds
1 garlic clove
40 g (1½ oz) pecorino
40 g (1½ oz) Parmesan
a good handful each of parsley and mint leaves
zest and juice of 1 large lemon, plus extra zest to serve
100 ml (3½ fl oz/scant ½ cup) extra virgin olive oil
100 g (3½ oz) per person pasta of your choice
sea salt

To roast the almonds, preheat the oven to 150°C fan (170°C/340°F). Spread out the almonds on a baking sheet and roast for about 12 minutes, until just toasty and beginning to smell good. Remove from the oven and set aside to cool slightly.

Blitz the garlic with the almonds and cheese in a food processor until they form a fine rubble. Add the herbs and the zest of the lemon (peeled in strips is fine if your food processor is vigorous, finely zested if not). Add the oil and blitz again. Taste for seasoning, adding salt and the juice of half the lemon. Keep tasting and adding more lemon juice or salt as necessary. It needs to be good and punchy as it will water down with the pasta, and a thick, creamy consistency (it will loosen up as you add the pasta water on cooking; if it looks too thick, let it down with a little more oil or water).

Cook the pasta in a large saucepan of boiling salted water until al dente, then drain and toss in the pesto, adding a good splash of the pasta cooking water and stirring until everything goes creamy.

Serve with some extra lemon zest on top.

Lemon & Fennel Risotto

A classic and elegant combination of the palest colour palette. This risotto is wonderful as it is, but if you'd like to gild the lily, you can add some sweet pink prawns (shrimp), or even better pale rose langoustines, or a handful of pebble-grey clams. I use a young Vernaccia as my wine of choice, but if gilding, you could use prosecco, in which case the dish becomes inevitably romantic, a Valentine's supper for two, maybe. Vermouth, with its slight oaky sweetness, is also delicious.

1 tablespoon olive oil
40 g (1⅓ oz/3 tablespoons) butter
1 small white onion, finely diced
1 small fennel bulb, finely diced, fronds reserved
160 g (5¾ oz/generous ¾ cup) risotto rice
125 ml (4 fl oz/½ cup) Vernaccia or vermouth
about 600 ml (20 fl oz/ 6½ cups) chicken or vegetable stock
2 tablespoons grated Parmesan
sea salt
finely grated zest and juice of 1 lemon

Heat the oil and half the butter in a large saucepan, add the onion and begin to soften over a low heat for around 10 minutes. Add the fennel and keep cooking until both soften and become translucent. Don't rush this bit as it's important to get the maximum flavour out of both vegetables.

Next, add the rice and stir for few minutes, then add the wine and allow to simmer for a few minutes as you stir. Now, add the stock, ladle by ladle, stirring well after each addition as the liquid is absorbed and the rice becomes creamy.

Once the rice is al dente and has absorbed most of the liquid, taste and test the rice for consistency (also add more liquid if you like it a little on the soupy side, as I do). It should take around 14–16 minutes to cook. Remove from the heat, add the remaining butter and beat in the cheese. Season with salt, to taste. Sprinkle with the finely grated lemon zest, then add a squeeze or two of the juice and serve, with the reserved fennel fronds scattered over.

Sea Bass Carpaccio with Citrus

SERVES 1

A pale fish carpaccio is somewhat a contradiction in terms as the dish derives its name from the red (raw beef) and white (mayonnaise) colours reminiscent of the Venetian painter Carpaccio. The original carpaccio is said to have been invented in Harry's Bar in Venice in 1950 by Giuseppe Cipriani to cater to the prescribed raw meat diet of Venetian countess Amalia Nani Mocenigo, but not wanting to simply present raw meat he livened it up with some drizzles of spiked white mayonnaise.

Carpaccio has come to refer to a number of dishes based around the concept of thinly sliced raw meat/fish/vegetables topped with some sort of salad/sauce combination. One of my favourite ways to begin a special meal is with fish carpaccio. Any form of citrus works well to garnish and prettify the dish (I recommend grapefruit segments, blood orange or lime), but the lemon juice, salt and olive oil are fundamental as they provide balanced flavour, depth and acidity, highlighting the sweetness and saltiness of the fish and also slightly curing it – just enough to firm up the flesh.

I like to use fresh sea bass fillet, but the recipe also works well with bass, bream, mullet, salmon, prawns (shrimp) or trout. Make sure you use very fresh fish.

1 small sea bass fillet or
  3 peeled and deveined raw
  prawns (shrimp) per person
½ orange, zested and then
  segmented
slivers of fresh chilli (optional)
a few delicate herbs of your
  choice (chervil, parsley, wild
  fennel, tarragon and/or dill
  all work)
a few edible flowers
radishes
juice of ½ lemon
2–3 tablespoons best-quality
  extra virgin olive oil
a good pinch of sea salt

Slice the fish into thin slivers and lay out flat on a plate.

Garnish with citrus segments and zest, perhaps a few slivers of fresh chilli and some delicate herbs. To finish, squeeze over a generous amount of lemon juice, drizzle over your best oil and sprinkle with some salt. (Also, I sometimes garnish with sliced radishes and edible flowers, if I have them.)

Serve and savour the simplest of flavours with a glass of something crisp and white or pink.

Baked Sardines

with Lemon & Parmesan Breadcrumbs

This is one of my mother-in-law's specialities, and a classic all over Italy. It is a lovely way of cooking any oily, full-flavoured fish, and of bulldozing the culinary myth that Italians never mix cheese with fish. Quick, cheap, nutritious and satisfying, it makes for a perfect simple supper or light lunch. Just add bread and a green salad.

This salty, herby, cheesy breadcrumb topping is a favourite for all kinds of seafood and vegetables (it's also very good with mussels and artichokes, for example). You can use either dried breadcrumbs or stale bread blitzed into crumbs.

250 g (9 oz) sardines
(3 small or 2 medium
sardines per person)
1 lemon
5 tablespoons fresh or dried
breadcrumbs
3 tablespoons olive oil, plus
extra for greasing
1 small garlic clove, grated
1 heaped tablespoon grated
Parmesan or pecorino
a few sprigs of parsley, leaves
roughly chopped
sea salt

Preheat the oven to 170°C fan (190°C/375°F). Grease a small ceramic baking dish with olive oil.

Butterfly the sardines. To do this, split them down their length, remove the backbones and heads, then press them open into flat double fillets. Place the sardines in the baking dish, skin side up and without layering them.

Zest half the lemon and then cut the lemon in half and squeeze the juice of one half into a bowl. Add the breadcrumbs, oil, grated garlic, lemon zest, cheese, chopped parsley and a good pinch or two of salt to the bowl and mix until you have a rough crumb. Cover the sardines with the crumb.

Cook in the oven for 10–12 minutes until the crumb is golden. Serve with the remaining lemon half cut into segments to garnish.

Salt Cod in Spiced Tomato Sauce with Capers & Lemon

Baccalà in Umido alla Sarda

This is a recipe from my favourite market stall, run by a husband-and-wife team who sell all kinds of delicious things (huge wheels of gently sweating pecorino, salted anchovies in giant tins, home-brined olives piled up in washing-up tubs and plastic bottles of rough local wine). Occasionally they display a few strips of what look like battered old plimsoll soles, but are in fact *baccalà*. *Baccalà* is a popular product all over Italy; the firm, meaty flesh of the cod makes it ideal for salting and preserving. Once soaked in fresh cold water, it swells and comes to life once more, to form a sweet, salty, fleshy fillet. While cod is not an indigenous fish, the salting means that it has travelled down into the cod-less Mediterranean kitchen, and become the protagonist of many an Italian dish.

It is a wonderful, undervalued ingredient, thrifty and delicious, and extremely versatile. Here, it is served in a piquant tomato sauce, which is made slightly sweet and sour and spicy, and served with some rather retro (but utterly essential) lemon pinwheels, which lend a lovely acidity and perfume. You can eat it hot, but actually (like the burrida, or seafood stew, popular here in Sardinia) it is almost more delicious cold, or at room temperature, on a hot summer's day, with some good bread for mopping up juices and a salad for after.

For this recipe, the salt cod needs to be soaked in lots of fresh cold water for 2 days, with the water changed at least a few times before it is ready to be used. If you can't find salt cod, you can also make this with any fresh white fish of your choice.

3 tablespoons olive oil, plus
  extra as needed
1 onion, thinly sliced
400 g (14 oz) salt cod, soaked
  (see introduction) and cut into
  4 pieces, or 4 white fish fillets
a pinch of dried chilli (hot
  pepper) flakes
1 x 400-g (14-oz) tin chopped
  tomatoes
a small glass of white wine
1½ teaspoons sugar
1 tablespoon capers
a handful of mixed olives
a good squeeze of lemon juice
s̶a̶l̶t̶
parsley or basil
  garnish
ls, to serve

Pour the oil into a large frying pan (skillet), add the onions and let them sweat gently, over a low heat, for about 10–15 minutes until they become completely soft and translucent and sweet. Remove them from the pan and set aside.

Add a glug more oil to the pan, add the cod, skin side down and sauté over a medium heat for a few minutes. Turn it over briefly to seal the other side, then turn it again to skin side down. Add back in the onions, along with the chilli flakes, tomatoes, wine and sugar and simmer for about 20 minutes until the cod is cooked and the sauce reduced. Throw in the capers and olives, taste and adjust the seasoning, adding a good squeeze of lemon juice.

Taste and add a pinch of salt if necessary (it's unlikely you'll need it), then serve with some chopped parsley or torn basil on top and a few lemon pinwheels.

Grilled Squid

with Lemon, Chilli, Rocket & Agrodolce Dressing

This is a delicious, fresh dressing that goes well with anything roasted, fried or grilled. I also highly recommend it with grilled courgettes (zucchini) or grilled salmon. If you like, you can blitz in a few fresh tomatoes, green olives, capers and/or anchovies.

Agrodolce vinegar is a white wine vinegar mixed with a little concentrated grape juice, to add sweetness and freshness. It is absolutely delicious in dressings, most specifically with fish. If you can't find it, use 1 tablespoon white wine vinegar and 1 teaspoon runny honey.

Serve with a sharp fennel salad.

4 medium squid

FOR THE DRESSING:
100 ml (3½ fl oz/scant ½ cup)
  olive oil
1–2 tablespoons agrodolce
  or white balsamic vinegar
zest of 1 lemon and juice of ½
½ garlic clove
a large handful of rocket
  (arugula) leaves
a pinch of dried chilli (hot
  pepper) flakes
a good pinch of sea salt

To clean the squid, pull the heads from the bodies and cut away the tentacles from the head and beak. Remove and discard the quill. Wash the squid under cold running water.

Blitz all of the ingredients for the dressing together in a food processor and taste for seasoning. Adjust as you see fit adding more salt, lemon or agrodolce (or honey).

Grill (broil), pan-fry or barbecue the squid pieces – the important thing is that they are cooked over a high heat and cooked until white and just caramelising at the edges of their bodies and tentacles. To serve, drizzle over the dressing.

Chicken, Honey & Preserved Lemon Tagine

SERVES 4–6

I once worked with an Israeli chef named Eyal who made the most delicious food I have ever tasted. He appeared for a few short weeks in the London restaurant where I worked, arriving from Thailand where he said he had 'discovered balance' (both metaphysical and culinary) and then disappeared just as quickly. The few times I managed to taste his food are some of my clearest and most abiding sensory memories.

Every time I tasted a dish made by him I would ask him what his secret was, and he would shrug and reply, purring through a provocative smile and emphasing his vowels for effect, 'butter, lemon and hoooney'. Eyal put butter, lemon and honey in almost everything he made, and he was alarmingly liberal with his spices and herbs. He would glide around the kitchen, his chef's trousers nearly around his knees and hanging from his slight frame, fishing a crisp from his pocket every now and then (he perennially had crisps in his pockets), and throw in a handful of whole chillies here, a huge whole bouquet – not bunch – of coriander (cilantro) there. Lemons roughly hacked into large pieces flew into the pot, alongside whole sticks of butter and jars of honey.

Eyal had no fear, and his curries and tagines were some of the deepest, most sweet, most sour, most rich, most fresh, most alive and most perfectly spiced and extraordinarily balanced dishes I have ever tasted. His three secret ingredients of butter, honey and lemon, in the correct quantities and settings, do blend to form a perfect sweet/sour/rich/ fresh/sharp/deep/mellow balance, and in this tagine I have tried to pay homage to him. I hope I have succeeded. Eat with some pocket crisps in his honour, or alternatively some nicely fluffy couscous and a sharp salad (I like a fennel, mint and orange salad with this).

2 tablespoons olive oil
1 tablespoon butter
6 chicken thighs or 1 whole
  chicken, jointed into 6 pieces
sea salt
2 white onions, thinly sliced
2 garlic cloves, thinly sliced
1 scant teaspoon ground
  turmeric
2 cinnamon sticks
1 teaspoon ground ginger
a good pinch of saffron threads
a large bunch of coriander
  (cilantro)
a handful of green olives, stone in
1 preserved lemon, flesh removed
  and discarded, rind cut into strips
250 ml (8 fl oz/1 cup) chicken
  stock or water
juice of 1 lemon
3 teaspoons runny honey

Heat the oil and butter in a deep flameproof casserole dish. Season the chicken pieces with salt, add to the casserole dish skin side down and begin to brown them over a medium heat (do this in batches to avoid overcrowding the dish). Once you have got a good colour all over each piece, remove from the dish and set aside.

Add a splosh more oil or a knob of butter if necessary, then add the onions to the dish. Cook them slowly, covered, until completely soft and translucent (at least 15–20 minutes). Add the garlic and spices and keep cooking for a few more minutes.

Separate the coriander leaves from the stems, roughly chop the leaves, and reserve for later. Finely chop the stems and add to the dish, stirring for a few minutes until they release their fragrance.

Now, add the chicken pieces back into the dish along with the olives, preserved lemon and chicken stock or water. Bring to the boil, then lower the heat to a steady simmer and cook,

covered, for about 35 minutes until the chicken is done
(the juices should run clear when the thickest part is pierced
with a sharp knife).

Taste for seasoning, add salt if necessary, reduce the sauce a
little if you like, then squeeze in the lemon juice and stir in the
honey. Taste again, adding more lemon, salt or honey to taste.
Finally, stir in the chopped coriander leaves and serve. Soft
flatbreads or couscous and salad are welcome additions.

Chicken Braised with Artichokes, Saffron & Lemon

A dish with Moroccan Jewish origins, this is a combination of three of my most favourite ingredients: chicken, artichokes and lemon. The original recipe also contained cinnamon, but I prefer it without. The saffron provides a subtle, almost sweet and honey-fragrant undernote that works well to counterbalance the sharpness of the lemon. A perfect late winter/early spring lunch or supper with flavours that succeed in being both deeply savoury and rich, and light and fresh, at the same time.

You can use chicken thighs for this or whole legs, depending on preference. Allow a leg or thigh per person. Serve with good bread, olive oil-roasted potatoes or a bitter leaf salad. Or all three.

4 chicken thighs or legs
sea salt
4 tablespoons extra virgin olive oil
240 ml (8 fl oz/1 cup) dry white wine (I use Vernaccia; dry sherry would also be good)
120 ml (4 fl oz/½ cup) chicken stock or water
1 white onion, thinly sliced
2 garlic cloves, thinly sliced
a good pinch of saffron threads
a large handful of parsley, roughly chopped
1 lemon, cut into 8 wedges
6–8 artichokes (prepped down to the hearts, then halved, see page 42)

Season the chicken pieces with salt. Warm half the oil in a heavy-based sauté pan or casserole dish (Dutch oven) and brown the chicken pieces (skin side down first). Without crowding the pan, aim to get a good light brown colour all over, then remove the pieces and set aside.

Deglaze the pan with a little of the wine or stock, scrape up all the good brown bits and save this liquid for later. Wipe out the pan briefly with a paper towel and place back over a low heat.

Warm the remaining oil in the same pan. Sauté the onion, garlic and saffron for 10–15 minutes until totally soft and translucent. Add half the chopped parsley and continue to cook for a few minutes. Add the lemon pieces and the artichokes and sauté for a minute or two longer, then add back in the chicken pieces (skin side up) with the wine, the reserved juices and the stock or water. Cover partially and cook for 25–30 minutes until the chicken is tender (the juices should run clear when the thickest part is pierced with a sharp knife) and the sauce is nicely reduced. Taste and check for seasoning, adding more salt if necessary. Serve with the remaining chopped parsley on top.

Lemon & Fennel Pork Meatballs

SERVES 4–6

A favourite simple supper; pork, fennel and lemon is a combination made in heaven. The key to good meatballs is to make them soft with the addition of bread soaked in milk and to create a deep and savoury flavour with good salty cheese. In this recipe, those elements are then perfectly counterbalanced by fragrant lemon and fennel. This makes about 30 mini meatballs or 18–20 larger, golf ball-sized ones. I have included a *bianco* (white) wine sauce below, but you can also serve these with your favourite tomato sauce (also spiked with some lemon zest).

100 ml (3½ fl oz/scant ½ cup) whole milk
3–4 slices (about 100 g/3½ oz) stale bread, crusts removed
500 g (1 lb 2 oz) minced (ground) pork
1 large egg
4 heaped tablespoons grated Parmesan or pecorino
1 teaspoon sea salt
zest of 1 large lemon
1 teaspoon fennel seeds, crushed
a good grating of nutmeg
250 ml (8 fl oz/1 cup) dry white wine
olive oil, for sautéing
bread, to serve

Preheat the oven to 160°C fan (180°C/350°F).

Pour the milk into a bowl, add the bread and soak until it has absorbed all the liquid and is completely soft. Mush it up between your fingers, then place in a bowl with the minced meat. Add the egg, cheese, salt, lemon zest, fennel seeds and nutmeg. Squidge everything together between your fingers until you have a smooth, even mix.

Shape the mixture into medium balls (sized according to preference) and place in a baking dish or on a baking tray. Cook on the hob using can use a frying pan (skillet) with a little oil and keep turning until they are cooked through.

Heat a little olive oil in a sauté pan over a medium heat and start to sauté the meatballs. Cook until you have some golden crusts forming, turning with a fork occasionally, then pour the white wine. Leave to simmer for a minute as the wine evaporates and then cover with a lid and cook over a gentle heat for 10–15 minutes, until the balls are cooked through and the wine has reduced to a nice consistency. Eat, with abundant bread for mopping up juices.

Lost in Leaves

Two

Grilled/Barbecued Mozzarella in Lemon Leaves

A staple of the Amalfi Coast that instantly sang its siren call to me (any form of cooked cheese is my idea of heaven; it must be that little – rare! – bit of Welsh in me), this is a lovely thing to cook on the barbecue, or failing clement weather under the grill (broiler)/in the oven/in a grill pan. Various cheeses are used, sometimes smoked mozzarella or scamorza, sometimes provolone, sometimes fresh mozzarella. Use whatever you can easily get hold of, or whatever takes your fancy. The leaves infuse their lemon-tree flavour into the cheese and, for this reason, I prefer a mild rather than a smoked cheese, as you can taste the fresh lemon flavour all the more.

about 16 lemon leaves
3 balls of good mozzarella
 or a chunk of provolone

Make sandwiches of thick slices of cold (and thus firm) cheese and lemon leaves (or rolls if doing on a barbecue, using cocktail sticks/toothpicks to hold in place) and then roast/grill/fry until the leaves have taken on colour and the cheese is melting. Eat the cheese but not the leaves.

Roasted Lemon-leaf Goat's Cheese

This is a dish that sings of the Mediterranean. The leaves impart a wonderful flavour and scent to the dish, the flavour a little like a fresh bay leaf mixed with lemon skin. You can use feta, halloumi, goat's cheese or a young pecorino – all work beautifully.

I hate writing recipes that are sunshine-specific, but even in drizzly places where perhaps lemons themselves are hard to find, if you know someone who has a tree you can ask for a few leaves. Or try to buy lemons with their leaves still attached, if you are lucky enough to find them.

3–4 lemon leaves
1 block of feta or cheese of your
    choice (about 150 g/5½ oz)
zest of 1 lemon and a squeeze
    of juice
1–2 tablespoons runny honey
flatbreads or focaccia, to serve

Preheat the oven to 180°C fan (200°C/400°F).

Wash the lemon leaves and place them in a small baking dish, then place the cheese on top. Roast in the oven for 8–10 minutes until golden at the edges and melting in the middle. Grate over some fresh lemon zest, drizzle over the honey and squeeze over a little juice, too, if you like. Serve with lots of crusty flatbread or focaccia and other snacking bits.

Baked, Breadcrumbed Lemon Leaf Chicken

SERVES 4–6

This has a whiff of the deliciousness of chicken Kyiv about it, but is made extra special by plenty of fresh herbs and both fresh lemon and lemon leaves. The lemon leaves infuse the meat with the most wonderful flavour, like standing next to a lemon tree on a hot day and inhaling, but if you can't find them, you can add a couple of lemon slices (the comfort for the cold-climate lemon grower is that even if you have no fruit, you can still cook with the leaves).

One of my favourite chicken recipes, the meat stays deliciously moist and perfumed, and the breadcrumbs oily and garlicky and delicious. It is extremely forgiving, too, as you can serve it in the same dish, and make it a little in advance as it holds well and does not dry out.

I like to use Vernaccia dry white wine in the marinade, but a dry sherry would also work well.

1 whole chicken, jointed, or 6 thighs, skin removed from all pieces
3 large glasses of dry white wine (half a bottle)
5 lemon leaves
2 garlic cloves
3 tablespoons olive oil, plus extra for drizzling
1 lemon
a few sprigs of parsley
1 fresh bay leaf
a sprig of rosemary
4 tablespoons breadcrumbs (either fresh or dried)
sea salt

Place the chicken in a suitable lidded container with the wine, one bashed garlic clove and a torn lemon leaf. Marinate overnight in the refrigerator (if not overnight then an hour beforehand – I often forget and do it for a half an hour or so, it will still help).

When ready to cook the chicken, preheat the oven to 160°C fan (180°C/350°F).

Line a deep roasting dish just large enough fit all the chicken with the remaining lemon leaves, then place the chicken on top (reserve the marinade for later). Drizzle over the olive oil.

Blitz the second garlic clove, 3 peeled strips of lemon zest, the parsley, bay leaf, rosemary and breadcrumbs until you have a crumb, then season with a good few pinches of salt. Coat the top of the chicken with the herby crumb and then drizzle over a little more oil and place in the oven. Cook for 30 minutes, then pour the marinade around the chicken pieces (not on top, otherwise your crispy breadcrumbs will go soggy).

Cook for another 20 minutes or so, until the chicken is cooked (check that the juices run clear when the thickest part is pierced with a knife), the marinade reduced and the crumb topping golden.

Serve, with the lemon cut into wedges to squeeze as you wish.

Sweet Lemons

Three

Soft & Chewy Lemon & Almond Biscuits

MAKES 30 BISCUITS

A classic almond sweet, or *dolci di mandorla*, but flavoured by lemon rather than bitter almonds, these are always popular with everyone, and make good gifts too. They are both gluten and dairy-free, and a doddle to make. You can keep them simple or decorate them with glacé (candied) cherries or crushed pistachios to provide more colour.

500 g (1 lb 2 oz/3¾ cups) whole blanched almonds, plus extra to decorate
zest of 1 large or 2 small lemons
400 g (14 oz/2 cups) caster (superfine) or granulated sugar
150 g (5½ oz) egg whites
icing (confectioner's) sugar, to decorate
glacé (candied) cherries, to decorate (optional)

Preheat the oven to 160°C fan (180°C/350°F). Line a large flat baking tray with baking parchment.

Grind the almonds, lemon zest and sugar in a food processor until they become a fine rubble. Pour into a bowl and add the egg white, little by little, until you have a soft dough. Mix with your hands. It should form a thick paste that is not runny, but slightly sticky.

Wet your hands slightly, then roll small golf ball-sized pieces. Place on the lined baking sheet and flatten them slightly with the palm of your hand. Press a whole almond or a glacé cherry into the top of each biscuit.

Bake in the oven for 13–15 minutes, until golden brown but still a little soft in the middle. Remove, allow to cool and then dust with icing sugar.

Lemon Bars with Polenta Pastry & Olive Oil Curd

The lemon bar is a teatime classic and the owner of one of the least romantic names in the history of food nomenclature. Despite its unjustly underwhelming name, this bar is delicious and delightful – a sort of lemon custard shortcake. Crumbly, buttery, creamy and tart, the sunshine-yellow squares are popular with both children and adults, and constitute an essential part of my Sardinian mother-in-law's grandly named, and even more grandly hosted, 'English teas'.

I have added polenta (cornmeal) to the pastry to Italianise them a bit, and also to add that pleasurable and grounding grittiness which works so well against the slick velvet of the curd. The curd itself is spiked with a little olive oil to make it extra glossy and provide the slightest peppery back note – a trick I gleaned from food writer Melissa Clark.

The method involves a few phases, but I assure you they are quick and painless.

FOR THE BASE:
100 g (3½ oz/¾ cup) plain (all-purpose) or 00 flour
60 g (2 oz/generous ⅓ cup) polenta (cornmeal)
120 g (4½ oz) butter
a good pinch of salt
zest of 1 lemon
80 g (2¾ oz/6 tablespoons) sugar

FOR THE CURD:
2 eggs plus 3 egg yolks
juice of 4 lemons
280 g (9¾ oz/1½ cups minus 2 tablespoons) sugar
10 g (½ oz/2 teaspoons) cornflour (cornstarch)
a pinch of salt
60 ml (2 fl oz/¼ cup) extra virgin olive oil
70 g (2½ oz) butter

icing (confectioner's) sugar, to decorate

Preheat the oven to 150°C fan (170°C/340°F). Line a 25 x 25 cm (10 x 10 in) brownie pan with baking parchment.

Blitz all the ingredients for the base in a food processor until you have a fine, damp sand. Press into the base of the tin, using the back of a spoon to form a flat, even layer. Bake in the oven for 20–30 minutes until golden all over and smelling biscuity.

Meanwhile, make the curd. Measure all the ingredients except the oil and butter directly into a saucepan, whisking until smooth. Cook over a medium heat, whisking continuously, until thick. The mixture should come to the boil and then begin to thicken after a few minutes. Remove from the heat and strain into a bowl. Whisk in the oil and the butter until smooth.

Pour the curd over the cooked base and then return to the oven and cook for a further 10–15 minutes, until just set.

Remove from the oven and allow to cool, then slice into squares, dust with icing sugar and serve.

Slightly Salty Lemon & Lavender Shortbread Biscuits

Based on a serendipitous bag of dainty French sablé that were melt-in-the-mouth, lemony and flecked with lavender, with the occasional welcome flake of French sea salt, these lovely, light biscuits (cookies) are so moreish you can eat twenty without thinking about it. Serve with a fragrant tea, such as Earl Grey. If you wish, cut these out using a double pastry cutter and sandwich them with either apricot or strawberry jam, both of which work beautifully with lavender and lemon. Or use some of your homemade lemon curd (page 122).

135 g (4¾ oz) unsalted butter
65 g (2¼ oz/generous ½ cup)
   icing (confectioner's) sugar
½ teaspoon sea salt
1 teaspoon dried or fresh
   lavender, crushed
zest of 1 lemon
150 g (5¼ oz/1 cup plus
   2 tablespoons) 00 flour
50 g (1¾ oz/½ cup) cornflour
   (cornstarch)

Preheat the oven to 140°C fan (160°C/325°F). Line a baking tray (pan) with baking parchment.

In a bowl, beat the butter with the icing sugar until light and fluffy. Beat in the salt, lavender and lemon zest, and finally the flours until you have a smooth dough (it will look crumbly at first, then come together as a smooth paste). Chill for at least 30 minutes.

Roll out the dough to a thickness of 1 cm (½ in) and stamp out cookies with a cutter of your choice (if making sandwich biscuits, make them thinner – roll to coin thickness in this case). Place on the lined baking tray.

Bake in the oven for 12–15 minutes until just golden around the edges, then remove from the oven and allow to cool on the tray.

Lemon & Elderflower Iced Buns

MAKES 12
BUNS

Every book I have ever written contains a bun recipe so, not wanting to break the habit, here is a lovely little lily-white iced (frosted) bun perfect for picnics, small people and parties, garnished with the delicate star-shaped flowers of elderflower. These are very good unfilled, but if you want to fill them then I have given you an option for the filling.

150 ml (5 fl oz/scant ⅔ cup) warm milk
100 ml (3½ fl oz/scant ½ cup) water
10 g (½ oz) fresh yeast
100 g (3½ oz/½ cup) sugar
10 g (½ oz/2 teaspoons) salt
560 g (1¼ lb/4¼ cups) plain (all-purpose) or 00 or bread flour
1 egg plus 1 egg yolk, plus beaten egg for brushing
70 ml (2½ fl oz/5 tablespoons) sunflower oil, plus extra for greasing
zest of 1 large lemon

FOR THE FILLING:
300 ml (10 fl oz/1¼ cups) double (heavy) cream
30 g (1 oz/3½ tablespoons) icing (confectioner's) sugar
a splash of elderflower cordial

FOR THE ICING:
150 g (5½ oz/1 cup) icing (confectioner's) sugar
lemon juice, as needed
fresh elderflowers, to decorate

Warm the milk in a small saucepan or microwave, then add the water to bring it to blood temperature or tepid. Mix in the yeast and sugar and whisk to dissolve.

Combine the salt and flour in a bowl. In a separate bowl, mix the whole egg and egg yolk, oil and lemon zest.

Mix the liquids into the flour, bringing everything together to form a sticky dough (use a mixer or your hands for this), then remove from the bowl and knead on a lightly oiled surface (you can do this whole process in a stand mixer if you have one). Knead for a few minutes until you have a smooth dough (the dough is sticky, so use a dough scraper, if you have one, to help you knead it and then scrape up bits from the surface).

Place the dough in a lightly oiled bowl and cover with cling film (plastic wrap). Leave in a warm place to rise for at least 1½ hours until doubled in size (or overnight in the refrigerator is even better).

Line a baking tray (pan) with baking parchment. Scrape the dough out of the bowl and, using a knife or dough cutter, divide it into 12 pieces, each weighing 80 g (2¾ oz), oiling your scales if necessary. Shape each piece into a neat round or sausage (there are good YouTube videos on how to do this) and then place on the lined baking tray, a few inches apart. Cover with an oiled plastic bag, making sure it does not touch the surface of the buns.

Leave them to prove for 1½ hours (they need to be in a warm, non-draughty spot) and double in size. Meanwhile, preheat the oven to 170°C fan (190°C/375°F).

Remove the bag from the buns and brush them evenly but gently all over with the beaten egg. Bake in the oven for 12–15 minutes until golden brown and risen.

Meanwhile, whip the cream and icing sugar to soft peaks and fold through the elderflower cordial.

Allow the buns to cool slightly before cutting a deep slit down the side and filling abundantly with whipped cream. Mix the icing sugar with enough lemon juice to form a thick icing, ice the buns, top with some fresh elderflowers and serve.

Two Perfect Pancakes

Classic Crêpes

The perfect flat pancake is eaten sprinkled with fresh lemon juice and sugar, and is probably the first thing many people learn to make on their own. When I was a child, the first thing I made with my mother were jam tarts, and the first thing I learnt how to make on my own were pancakes. I made myself pancakes for breakfast every day for about two years, between the ages of nine and eleven. They are an example of the simplest ingredients used well and served with the simplest seasonings. Historically, we always had ours with Jif lemon, which I loved (page 7) but now I am spoilt for citrus.

The ratio and method are the same as I have always used for Yorkshire pudding (a giant, flabby yet crisp pancake relative, cooked in beef dripping if you're lucky). One egg per person, enough flour whisked in until it becomes almost too thick to whisk, then let down with milk until the consistency of single (light) cream. A little salt should be added, as well as some of the melted butter from the frying pan (skillet).

I never follow measurements, but for precise cooks or beginners, follow the quantities below.

2 eggs
120 g (4½ oz/scant 1 cup) plain
  (all-purpose) or 00 flour
  (I use farro)
190 ml (6¾ fl oz/¾ cup)
  whole milk
sea salt
1 tablespoon butter, melted,
  plus extra for frying

TO SERVE:
1 fresh lemon, halved
2 tablespoons sugar
  (of your choice – I like
  granulated for grit)

Break the eggs into a bowl and whisk to break them up. Gradually whisk in the flour until smooth, then slowly whisk in the milk until runny and smooth. Mix in a good pinch or two of salt and the melted butter. Ideally, allow the batter to rest for around 20 minutes, but you can use it straight away.

Melt a little butter in your favourite pancake pan. Pour in a ladleful of the batter, lifting the pan and swirling it around to get a large disc. Cook on one side for 2–3 minutes until just golden brown, then flip it over and cook the second side for another 2–3 minutes until golden. Slide on to a plate and serve with lemon and sugar.

Tradition says the first pancake is never completely successful (in our house the first one is always for the dog or the chickens), but the second one will be great.

Scotch Ricotta

A favourite tea at my grandmother's house were the Scotch pancakes she cooked directly on her range, then wrapped in a dish towel to keep warm before bringing the steaming bundle to us children waiting hungrily at the table. Floppy, sweet, with just the faintest background note of bicarbonate of soda (baking soda) and washing powder (from said dish towel), we ate them slathered with salty butter and her tooth-achingly sweet homemade Alpine strawberry jam.

Pancakes do not exist in Italy, except by enthusiastic introduction from nostalgic foreigners such as myself, and these ricotta pancakes have become a family favourite. The trick is to use more ricotta than flour, so they stay extra light and fluffy. Plenty of lemon zest roots them firmly in the Mediterranean and miles away from my granny's cold kitchen. I like them with yoghurt and homemade jam or honey.

You can keep these and eat them the next day – they stay good and moist.

300 g (10½ oz) ricotta
(tub or fresh)
2 eggs
100 g (3½ oz/¾ cup) plain
(all-purpose) or OO flour
(I use farro)
1½ tablespoons sugar
(optional)
zest of 1 lemon
a good pinch of salt
160 ml (5½ fl oz/⅔ cup)
whole milk
3 teaspoons baking powder
butter or oil, for frying
jam (preserves), honey, yoghurt
and/or fresh fruit, to serve

Place the ricotta in a bowl and whisk in the eggs until smooth. Add the flour and whisk again to form a thick paste. Add the sugar (if using), lemon zest, salt and milk (a bit at a time is easier) and whisk well until you have a batter that looks a bit like the consistency of crème fraîche (it will be slightly grainy, but that's fine). Finally, whisk in the baking powder.

Heat a little butter or oil in a frying pan (skillet) and add large scoops (about 2–3 tablespoons per pancake) of the mixture to make pancakes. Cook for 2 or 3 minutes on each side until brown.

Damp Lemon, Olive Oil & Fennel Seed Tea Cake

Many of the flavour pairings that work so well in a savoury context work equally well in a sweet one. A lemony tea cake soaked in syrup and flecked with fennel seeds is a play on two of the most traditional English tea cakes – caraway and lemon drizzle. The fennel adds a lovely sweet-aniseed lift to this unapologetically damp cake that is perfect with a cup of Earl Grey tea.

I like the combination of olive oil and butter in cakes, partly because it feels appropriate to my Italian/English way of cooking, and partly because both contribute their unique qualities to the flavour and texture. The oil gives the cake the palest green tinge and makes it extra light and moist, as well as providing a rich, grassy depth of flavour which works perfectly with the lemon and fennel seeds.

As with all citrus cakes, you can keep them plain and simple or soak them in a drizzle, and then also top with a simple lemon glaze if you like. With this particular cake, for everyday eating I like it either plain or drizzled, but a simple, pale white icing (frosting) dripping down the sides provides a lovely aesthetic if making it for a special occasion.

120 g (4½ oz) butter, plus extra for greasing
180 g (6½ oz/1 cup minus 1½ tablespoons) sugar
a good pinch of salt
zest of 2 lemons
80 ml (2¾ fl oz/ 5½ tablespoons) extra virgin olive oil
3 eggs
100 g (3½ oz/¾ cup) plain (all-purpose) or 00 flour
100 g (3½ oz/1 cup) ground almonds (almond meal)
3 teaspoons baking powder
60 ml (2 fl oz/¼ cup) milk
2 teaspoons fennel seeds (try to find nice green fresh ones), slightly crushed, plus extra to decorate

FOR THE SYRUP:
100 g (3½ oz/½ cup) sugar
juice of 2 lemons

Preheat the oven to 150°C fan (170°C/340°F). Grease a large loaf tin and line with baking parchment.

Beat the butter, sugar, salt, lemon zest and olive oil in a bowl until fluffy. Gradually beat in the eggs, then add the flour, ground almonds and baking powder and mix until smooth. Finally, beat in the milk and fennel seeds.

Pour into the prepared loaf tin. Bake in the oven for 40–50 minutes, or until a skewer inserted into the centre comes out clean.

To make the syrup, warm the sugar with the lemon juice in a saucepan until dissolved. Remove the cake from the oven and drizzle the syrup over the top while it is still warm.

Allow to cool, then serve with some extra fennel seeds on top, or ice with a simple glaze and extra fennel seeds.

Lemon, Yoghurt & Semolina Cake with Elderflower Drizzle

Elderflower and lemon is a classic flavour combination that reminds me of my English home and many years of making and drinking lemony elderflower cordial with my granny. The first elderflower blooms in Italy during peak lemon season, in mid-April, and making a floral-scented drizzle for this moist cake is a wonderful way of using both ingredients.

The semolina is a nod to the Sardinian (and southern Italian) tradition of using semola in cakes, which makes them extra light, moist and golden. Unlike polenta, it does not provide a sandy texture, its presence is more subtle but just as welcome. It makes the cake extra fluffy (think of how fluffy well-made couscous is – also made from semola). This is a good pudding cake.

2 eggs
200 ml (7 fl oz/scant 1 cup) plain yoghurt
60 ml (2 fl oz/¼ cup) whole milk
60 ml (2 fl oz/¼ cup) neutral oil, such as sunflower oil
220 g (8 oz/1 cup plus 2 tablespoons) sugar
zest of 1 large lemon
150 g (5½ oz/1 cup plus 2 tablespoons) plain (all-purpose) or 00 flour
100 g (3½ oz/¾ cup) semolina
3 teaspoons baking powder
1 teaspoon salt

FOR THE DRIZZLE:
40 g (1½ oz/3¼ tablespoons) sugar
juice of ½ lemon
blossoms from a couple of heads of elderflower or some elderflower cordial

Preheat the oven to 160°C fan (180°C/350°F). Grease a round 23 cm (9 in) cake tin (pan) and line with baking parchment.

Whisk the wet ingredients together in a bowl. Combine all the dry ingredients in a separate bowl, then gently whisk the dry ingredients into the wet ingredients until you have a smooth batter.

Pour into the prepared tin. Bake in the oven for 40 minutes, or until a skewer inserted into the centre comes out clean. Remove from the oven.

To make the drizzle, combine the sugar and lemon juice in a small saucepan and heat gently to dissolve. Add the blossom of a couple of heads of elderflower (shake them from their stems), then pour over the cake whilst still warm. Allow to cool completely before serving.

Lemon & Coconut Cream Cake

SERVES 8-10

There is something extremely chic about this cake, like a very fine, cream alpaca cardigan. The crumb is extra tender and delicately sweet thanks to the coconut cream, and the fragrant zest cuts through everything nicely. It would work well as a sandwich cake, too. I like it as a summer breakfast, or for a celebratory tea.

225 g (8 oz) unsalted butter, softened
200 g (7 oz/1 cup) sugar
4 eggs
1 teaspoon salt
zest of 2 lemons
3 teaspoons baking powder
250 g (9 oz/2 cups) plain (all-purpose) or 00 flour
200 ml (7 fl oz/scant 1 cup) coconut cream

FOR THE TOPPING:
40 g (1½ oz/1 cup) coconut flakes, to decorate
170 g (6 oz) mascarpone
100 ml (3½ fl oz/scant ½ cup) coconut cream
50 g (1¾ oz/generous ⅓ cup) icing (confectioner's) sugar
a few drops of vanilla extract
zest of 1 lemon, to decorate

Preheat the oven to 160°C fan (180°C/350°F). Grease and line a 20 cm (8 in) cake tin (pan).

Beat the butter with the sugar in a bowl until light and fluffy. Beat in the eggs one at a time, then the salt, lemon zest and baking powder. Finally, beat in the flour and the coconut cream until you have a smooth batter.

Pour into the prepared tin and bake in the oven for 45–55 minutes, or until a skewer inserted into the centre comes out clean. Remove from the oven and allow to cool in the tin.

Lightly toast the coconut flakes in a small frying pan over the lowest heat (keep an eye on them; they burn very quickly!) until just golden around the edges. Set aside.

Whip the mascarpone, coconut cream, icing sugar and vanilla extract together and, once the cake is completely cool, ice it and top with the toasted coconut flakes and lemon zest.

Lemon & Almond Layered Celebration Cake

I'm not usually a triple-layered-cake kind of person, mostly because my maleficent oven can't even cook one cake properly, so three would be asking a lot. However, if you have a more forgiving oven (I use my mother-in-law's) then you can easily bake three cakes at once, and make a spectacular, triple-layered birthday cake.

This was my memorable birthday cake in 2022, made by brilliant cook Allegra D'Agostini, and it actually made me cry a little. It was also my birthday cake in 2024, when we shot this book. I like commemorative cakes. Something about a third layer just shouts celebration. And three layers of cake also means three layers of cream. The cake is made by reverse creaming (something I had never heard of before Allegra introduced me to it, but it makes for a lovely, soft and moist crumb, and is satisfying to do).

½ teaspoon salt
90 g (3¼ oz/scant 1 cup) ground almonds (almond meal)
310 g (10¾ oz/2¼ cups) plain (all-purpose) or 00 flour
3 teaspoons baking powder
250 g (9 oz/1¼ cups) sugar
zest of 1 large lemon
200 g (7 oz) unsalted butter, at room temperature
210 g (7½ oz) egg whites (from 7 large eggs)
275 ml (9 fl oz/1⅛ cups) whole milk, at room temperature
a few edible flowers, to serve

FOR THE CREAM:
400 ml (14 fl oz/generous 1½ cups) whipping cream
4 tablespoons icing (confectioner's) sugar
½ teaspoon vanilla extract or bean paste
200 ml (7 fl oz/scant 1 cup) plain yoghurt

FOR THE STRAWBERRIES:
300 g (10½ oz) strawberries
zest and juice of 1 lemon
1 tablespoon sugar
a few drops of rose water

Preheat the oven to 160°C fan (180°C/350°F). Grease three identical 23 cm (9 in) cake tins (pans) and line with baking parchment.

Mix together the salt, ground almonds, flour, baking powder and sugar in the bowl of a stand mixer. Add the lemon zest. At medium speed, mix in the butter, a tablespoon at a time, until the mixture looks like damp sand.

In a separate bowl, whisk together the egg whites and milk to combine. Add this liquid mixture to the dry almond mixture, one half at a time, mixing as you go. Beat until light and airy.

Divide the batter evenly between the prepared tins. Bake in the oven for 30–35 minutes, or until a skewer stuck into the centre comes out clean. Remove and allow to cool before removing from the tins.

Meanwhile, whip the cream with the icing sugar until it forms soft peaks, then add the vanilla, and finally, gently fold in the yoghurt.

Hull the strawberries and place them in a bowl with the lemon zest and juice, sugar and rose water. Leave to marinate for a minute or two.

Assemble the cakes with layers of cream between, then top with the strawberries and edible flowers and serve.

Almond & Lemon Praline

Gattò

A classic sweet of Sardinia, and one of the best (practical and culinary) uses of lemon I know, there is something wonderfully restrained and minimalistic, yet inherently practical and canny, about this very particular *dolce*. Mentioned by Grazia Deledda (Sardinia's most famous author and winner of the Nobel Prize in Literature), it is one of the most traditional sweets of Sardinia and, like so many of its relatives, it is incredibly simple and contains only three ingredients, two of which form the pillars of the Sardinian sweet kitchen: almonds and lemons.

Presented in shining caramel-coloured diamonds on waxy green lemon leaves (which provide a handy decorative and biodegradable plate), it is a classic at any celebratory event, and is popular with adults and children alike. Both the almonds and the lemons are usually homegrown.

Here, the lemon is used to moisten the surface before spreading out the praline (thus preventing it from sticking, but flavouring it too) and then a cut half is passed over the hot surface, to flatten it and perfume it once again. The equal quantity of almonds and sugar means that the nut is as important as the sugar, and it should be nicely toasty, as, along with the lemony undertones, this ensures the *gattò* is not too sweet.

It's a fun thing to make with children if you make sure little hands are protected from hot praline with halved lemons; there is something rather reminiscent of potato stamping in the use of a cut lemon as a tool.

300 g (10½ oz/2¼ cups)
 blanched almonds
300 g (10½ oz/1½ cups) sugar
1 lemon, halved
a pinch of salt
lemon leaves (you can also
 use bay leaves if you prefer)

Preheat the oven to 150°C fan (170°C/340°F). Spread the almonds out on a baking tray (pan) and toast in the oven for 14–16 minutes until pale caramel colour and smelling delicious. Remove from the oven, allow to cool and then chop them into slivers if you have time, or rough chunks if you don't (they look prettier nibbed but it's time-consuming).

Make a dry caramel by melting the sugar in a deep saucepan over a high heat, swirling it occasionally until you have a clear, shiny, liquid caramel. Just as it begins to smoke, add the almonds and salt, stirring well to coat.

Rub one of the lemon halves all over a smooth, clean surface (a wooden or marble work surface is best) and pour over the praline, spreading it out flat with the other lemon half.

Cut the praline into diamond-shaped pieces while it is still warm. Allow to cool completely before serving on the lemon or bay leaves.

Note: You can also use this as a traditional praline, and break it up into shards to decorate puddings such as panna cotta (page 156) or stick a slab into creamy ice cream (page 183).

Triflettes

Almost an Italian version of the traditional Scottish cranachan dessert, these are lovely, easy, delicious and creamy mini layered trifles or 'triflettes', which involve minimal preparation. I love the notion of an English trifle, 'just a trifle', here 'just a triflette'. But a trifle is never just a trifle: it is the perfect holy trinity of cake/biscuit (cookie), cream and sharp fruit. I often buy frozen mixed berries, but if you have good fresh ones, lucky you. Raspberries on their own are also good. You can douse the biscuits in a little amaretto if you like, for extra almond flavour.

FOR THE BERRY SYRUP:
250 g (9 oz) fresh or frozen
   raspberries
4–5 tablespoons sugar
   (depending on the sweetness
   of your berries)
zest and juice of ½ lemon

**FOR THE LEMON
RICOTTA CREAM:**
250 g (9 oz) ricotta (a tub is fine)
3 tablespoons icing
   (confectioner's) sugar
400 ml (14 fl oz/generous
   1½ cups) double (heavy)
   cream
zest of 1 lemon
a few drops of vanilla extract

FOR THE CRUMBLE LAYER:
140 g (5 oz) cantucci/hard
   amaretti or biscuits (cookies)
   of your choice, crushed

TO DECORATE:
toasted flaked (slivered)
   almonds or pistachios
sprigs of mint
lemon zest

Put the berries into a saucepan with a splash of water, the sugar and lemon zest. Cook briefly over a gentle heat until exploding and syrupy. Add a squeeze of the lemon juice and set aside to cool.

Whip the ricotta with the icing sugar, then whip in the cream, lemon zest and vanilla until it forms soft, smooth peaks.

Crush the biscuits into a rough crumb.

Layer up the trifles in individual glasses, with biscuit first, then berry syrup, then cream. Top with toasted flaked almonds, sprigs of mint and lemon zest, and serve.

Ginger, Honey & Lemon Brandy Snaps

Brandy snaps were one of my favourite things as a child, the caramel-coloured, sticky, ginger-and-lemon scented tubes stuffed with whipped cream to become that beguiling mixture of crisp and chewy at the same time. The Italians have cannoli, another tube-shaped sweet filled with a creamy substance, which is equally delicious. This recipe is a happy hybrid of the two, which plays heavy on the lemon and ginger flavours and substitutes the traditional (and hard to find in Italy) golden syrup with honey.

These are equally popular with children and adults. If making them in the summer, substitute the stem ginger with crushed pistachios and serve with a big bowl of fresh raspberries. They are also very good with shards of dark chocolate stirred through the cream (cannoli style), or the tubes themselves half dunked in melted dark chocolate before being filled… I could go on.

Making perfect tubes requires a little practise, but even imperfect ones taste good. You can also buy ready-made brandy snaps if you are short of time and use this filling.

50 g (1¾ oz) unsalted butter
50 g (1¾ oz/¼ cup) demerara sugar
50 g (1¾ oz/3 tablespoons) honey
a pinch of salt
50 g (1¾ oz/heaping ⅓ cup) plain (all-purpose) or 00 flour, sifted
½ teaspoon ground ginger
zest of ½ lemon
1 teaspoon lemon juice

FOR THE FILLING:
350 ml (8 fl oz/1 cup) double (heavy) cream
zest of ½ lemon
2½ tablespoons icing (confectioner's) sugar
30 g (1½ oz) stem ginger in syrup, chopped into small pieces

Preheat the oven to 160°C fan (180°C/350°F). Line two or three large baking sheets with baking parchment.

Place the butter, sugar, honey and salt in a saucepan and warm over a low heat until the butter and sugar have melted.

Put the flour and ground ginger into a bowl and add the lemon zest. Add the lemon juice to the liquid in the saucepan, then add the liquid into the dry ingredients, mixing well until smooth. Place teaspoons of the mixture a few inches apart (they spread out enormously) onto the prepared baking sheets.

Bake in the oven for 8–9 minutes, until the biscuits are caramel brown and lacy-looking, making sure not to overcook them as the sugar burns and they become bitter.

Remove from the oven and wait a minute or two until they are cool enough to handle but still bendy (they should be hot but not burning) and then shape them around a thick pre-oiled handle (a wooden spoon is traditional but you can use an oiled cannoli tube). Wrap them around the handle/tube, press to stick together forming a neat tube, then slide gently off. Allow to cool completely before filling.

To make the filling, whip the cream with the icing sugar and some syrup from the ginger in a bowl. Use a piping (pastry) bag or knife to fill the tubes and then sprinkle with the stem ginger and serve. These soften a little if left in the refrigerator over time but that – at least for me – is no bad thing.

Allegra's Whole Lemon Ciambellone

I find that just like dogs, recipes often resemble their owners. This is a recipe that, like its owner Allegra, manages to be simultaneously homely in its goodness and yet somehow glamorous too, in an understated way. Like some of the best citrus cake recipes of all time (think Claudia Roden's seminal whole orange cake), it involves a whole blitzed fruit in the mixture.

It is a cake designed for breakfast: not too sweet or rich, instead springy, moreish and with a lovely lemony flavour and slight chewiness to it, like good breakfast muffins. It is best the day after it is made. Use your favourite ciambellone or ring/bundt mould.

5 eggs, separated
270 g (9¾ oz/1½ cups minus 2 tablespoons) sugar
1 medium lemon
100 ml (3⅓ fl oz/scant ½ cup) olive oil
50 ml (1¾ fl oz/ 3½ tablespoons) milk
250 g (9 oz/1¾ cups plus 2 tablespoons) plain (all-purpose) or 00 flour, plus extra for dusting
3 teaspoons baking powder
butter or oil, for greasing
icing (confectioner's) sugar, for dusting

Preheat the oven to 160°C fan (180°C/350°F). Grease your favourite ciambellone/bundt/cake mould well (paint the creases with melted butter or oil) and dust with flour.

Whip the yolks using a hand-held whisk or stand mixer with the sugar until thick and moussey. Cut the lemon into quarters, remove any obvious pips and blitz in a food processor until it forms a pulp. Add the oil and milk to the lemon and the whipped yolks. Stir in the flour and the baking powder.

Whip the egg whites to soft peaks and fold them into the mixture gently, starting with one or two spoonfuls to lighten the mixture before carefully folding in the rest. It will look lovely and foamy once the whites have been incorporated. Decant into your prepared mould.

Bake in the oven for around 45 minutes until a skewer inserted into the centre comes out clean.

Allow to cool and then turn out. Dust with icing sugar and serve.

A
zest
FOR
LIFE

The Use of Zest in Cooking

The zest of a lemon is a well-appreciated ingredient in the pastry kitchen, but perhaps less so in savoury cooking. The aromatic oils in the zest lend a fragrance and flavour to cake and pastry doughs, batters, ice creams and sorbets, and chime beautifully in sweet scenarios with spices such as saffron and cardamom, and essences such as rose and orange blossom, but I would make a case for lemon zest in a savoury context too. Finely grated lemon zest works beautifully tossed through most salads or cooked vegetables, as well as in dressings, sauces and salsas. Try adding it to savoury pastries, stirring it into dressings, or scattering it over roasted vegetables together with finely grated Parmesan. It makes a lovely balanced way of dressing numerous leaves (cooked and raw), the caramel sweetness and savoury depth of the cheese being perfectly offset by the aromatic zest. In some salads and other savoury scenarios I like to use whole pieces of lemon (finely chopped) to get the simultaneous hit of acidic juice and fragrant zest in one mouthful.

LEMON ON MEAT

While lemon is not welcome on every meat (roast beef, for example), it can beautifully counteract the fatty flavour of many cooked cuts (and raw meat, too – a traditional raw beef carpaccio is always seasoned with lemon juice, as is tartare). I particularly like lemon juice on grilled or fried cuts of pork and veal, and with chicken cooked in almost any way. The intensely rich flavour of lamb works especially well with lemon, too, whether the fresh juice or the fragrant zest.

LEMON ON FISH

Of course it goes without saying that many people love to squeeze a fresh lemon wedge over their fish fillet, or slip a sliver into a whole fish's belly as it bakes. But as with all cooking, the devil is in the detail, and there are moments when a lemon is best seized and put to immediate use, or left shining and expectant in its bowl. It very much depends on the fish. If you have an oily fish, like mackerel, mullet or sardine, I would be in favour of perfuming the flesh with some citrus. If you are lucky enough to have a fresh bass or bream, I like to taste their delicate, sweet flesh without any lemon at all. The same goes for shellfish – I like the sweet and briny delicacy of shellfish without any lemon, which can be harsh in such circumstances. The cooking method often determines lemon usage, too; the smoky flavour of grilled fish needs lemon to cut and correct, as does the salty fat of fried fish. An oven-roasted bream with herbs and olive oil is happy left un-lemoned, as is braised or boiled white fish. Salmon and trout are so rich and fatty I would almost always serve them with lemon.

LEMON ON FRIED THINGS

Many, though not all, fried things benefit from a squeeze of lemon to cut through the salty fat of the crispy batter or crust. The juice must be administered at the last minute, to make sure the batter does not become soggy, but otherwise it is very much a question of personal preference. In my English past, I never added vinegar to my fish and chips, and I don't often add lemon to my fried calamari now, it depends on how fresh they are, and what mood I'm in. There is no denying that a squeeze of lemon on a hot fried thing can be delicious.

LEMON ON CHEESE

Cheese and lemon are a natural combination. The fattiness of cheese – especially when cooked and, most specifically, fried – is cut through by lemon juice. Many sheep's cheeses (and also plenty of goat's cheeses, too) have an inherently lemony flavour that can be beautifully picked out by the addition of a little juice or rind.

LEMON IN BAKED GOODS

It is hard to think of baking without lemon zest, which is to my sweet pantry even more essential than vanilla. A little lemon zest lifts a cake batter or biscuit dough, and the juice is essential for finishing syrups and icings. In Sardinia, it is common to dry citrus rinds over the fire for use in *dolci* even when they are no longer readily available, so essential is citrus to the making of sweets. Italian creams or custards are almost always flavoured with lemon, which gives them a distinctive and instantly recognisable flavour and scent.

LEMON IN POACHING FRUIT

Unless I am specifically making an orange-flavoured sweet, I almost always poach my fruit with a strip or two of lemon zest. When added to a poaching syrup it brings out the best in the fruit.

LEMON IN MACERATING FRESH FRUIT

As with poaching, so with raw fruit. If your fruit is not perfect as it is, macerating it for a few minutes in a little lemon juice and sugar can elevate it enormously. The lemon juice also slightly 'cooks' the fruit, softening hard or underripe strawberries, for example.

Lemon Panna Cotta with Strawberries

The simplest of puddings, and still one of the best. This is my classic ratio, but infused with a little lemon zest. I use the barest minimum of gelatine to make for the very softest wobble. Use dainty ramekins or espresso cups as moulds.

400 ml (14 fl oz/generous 1½ cups) double (heavy) cream
100 ml (3½ fl oz/scant ½ cup) milk
50 g (1¾ oz/¼ cup) sugar
1 vanilla pod (bean), split
3–4 g (¹/₈ oz or 2 leaves) gelatine
3 strips of lemon zest

TO SERVE:
500 g (1 lb 2 oz) strawberries, hulled
zest and juice of ½ lemon
1–2 tablespoons sugar
a few lemon blossoms, if you can find them, or other edible flowers

Warm half the cream in a saucepan with the milk, sugar and vanilla pod over a low-medium heat and bring to scalding point.

Soak the gelatine in a small bowl of cold water and allow to soften completely (around a minute).

Squeeze out and add the softened gelatine to the hot cream mixture and stir well to dissolve. Add the remaining cream to the mixture and strain it, discarding the vanilla pod (save this to use in another recipe).

Decant into your preferred moulds and place in the refrigerator to set for at least 4 hours. Ideally, remove from the refrigerator around 15 minutes before serving to take the chill off.

Meanwhile, marinate the strawberries in the lemon juice, zest and sugar. To serve, top the panna cottas with the strawberries and flowers.

Milk Tart

Flan di Latte

This is a beloved Sardinian childhood classic that tends to be loved just as fervently by nostalgic adults. 'Flan', states the *Oxford Companion to Sugar and Sweets*, 'is most often associated with Spain and the countries it traded with during the early era of sea exploration.' Therefore, it seems more than likely that this dessert is an inheritance from the Spanish rule of Sardinia. Much like crème caramel it is a baked custard, but differs in its lighter, more delicate texture and flavour. Unlike crème caramel, it is flavoured with lemon rather than vanilla and uses only milk and no cream. It takes mere minutes to throw together.

Light, lemony, milky-sweet and just wobbling, I like it made in a large dish and eaten in wibbling scoops that collapse on the plate at the touch of a spoon. I don't bother turning it out as an elegant crème caramel, as one of its unpretentious charms is that once you break the pristine surface for the first time, it collapses into quivering, craggy pieces, which bob and duck about on a liquid sea of caramel like precarious primrose-coloured icebergs.

We like it especially at breakfast the day after, eaten cold from the refrigerator with a teaspoon and a hot black coffee.

4 egg yolks
500 ml (17 fl oz/2 cups)
 whole milk
a few strips of lemon zest
100 g (3½ oz/½ cup) sugar

FOR THE CARAMEL:
70 g (2½ oz/scant ⅓ cup)
 sugar

Preheat the oven to 160°C fan (180°C/350°F) and place a deep baking dish filled with hot water (to make a bain-marie) inside.

Heat the milk in a saucepan with the lemon zest and sugar until just scalding, then whisk it into the egg yolks. Remove the strips of lemon zest and discard.

Now, make the caramel. Heat the sugar in a pan over a high heat, swirling the pan occassionally, until just beginning to smoke and turning a pale coffee colour, then pour it into your chosen milk tart dish. Next, pour in the custard mixture and place gently into the bain-marie in the oven.

Bake for 45 minutes until just set. Remove from the bain-marie to stop it cooking and allow to cool. Serve cold.

Lemon-scented Crema Catalana

The *crema catalana* is another traditional Sardinian pudding based upon a simple cooked custard, though this version is richer and more refined than the milkily innocent and humble Milk Tart (page 158). The quantities are roughly the same, but using cream rather than milk makes things extra indulgent. Topped with a crunchy layer of caramelised sugar, it is very similar to crème brûlée, but arrived in Sardinia via the Catalan influence, and thus is flavoured with the more traditional cinnamon and lemon zest, rather than vanilla. Many versions include cornflour (cornstarch) but I make it without, and I top it with demerara sugar as a nod to my grandmother's crème brûlée – it makes an extra crunchy, toffee-ish crust. You can use a fancy blowtorch for burning your sugar topping, but if you don't have one, worry not – my granny always did it very effectively under the grill (broiler). You can use ramekins or tea cups as the moulds.

4 egg yolks
100 g (3½ oz/½ cup) sugar
500 ml (17 fl oz/2 cups) double
   (heavy) cream
1 cinnamon stick
1 strip of lemon zest
6 teaspoons demerara sugar

Preheat the oven to 140°C fan (160°C/325°F) and place a deep baking dish filled with hot water (to make a bain-marie) inside.

Whisk the egg yolks with the sugar with a hand whisk. Warm the cream in a saucepan with the cinnamon stick and strip of lemon zest until just beginning to boil, then whisk it into the egg yolk mixture. Remove the lemon and cinnamon and decant into your chosen ramekins. Place them in the bain-marie in the oven and cook for 40–50 minutes, until just set.

Remove from the bain-marie and allow to cool completely, before topping with each ramekin with a teaspoon of demerara sugar. Place under a hot grill (broiler) until desired coloured or caramelise with a blowtorch.

Lemon Possets in Lemon Boats

When you are lucky enough to have beautiful, leafy lemons, there is no nicer thing than halving them, scooping out the flesh (to squeeze) and filling them with lemon posset. The flavour of the rind perfumes the posset and provides a perfect picturesque vessel.

You will need to scoop out four whole lemons, to create the 'boats' this is served in, but you only use the juice of two, so the pulp from the others can be used in another recipe.

90 ml (3 fl oz/generous
⅓ cup) lemon juice
(I use 2 large lemons)
400 ml (14 fl oz/generous
1½ cups) double (heavy)
cream
90 g (3 oz/½ cup minus
1 tablespoon) sugar
8 hollowed-out lemon halves,
to serve

Combine the cream and sugar in a saucepan and bring to a low boil. Stir gently (the cream will expand a lot) and continue to cook for a minute or two, making sure the sugar has dissolved.

Remove from the heat, and allow to cool for a few minutes.

Add the lemon juice to the cream mixture, then decant into your lemon boats. (Note: the boats need to be on a flat surface so the liquid doesn't spill.)

Chill in the refrigerator for at least 2 hours, or overnight.

Instant Lemon & White Chocolate Mascarpone Mousse

I don't often use white chocolate in recipes, and on its own I find it too rich and sweet, but matched with tart berries and aromatic lemon zest it works beautifully. This is the only white chocolate mousse recipe I have ever come across that does not involve eggs. You could also spin it into a sort of *tiramisù* or trifle and add some sweet wine or milk-soaked trifle sponges or crushed biscuits between the layers. You could also pipe the mousse, as shown, to make beautiful mounds.

The red, white and green perfectly mirror the Italian flag.

100 g (3½ oz) white chocolate
200 ml (7 fl oz/scant 1 cup) whipping cream, at room temperature
zest of 1 lemon, plus extra to serve
100 g (3½ oz/½ cup) mascarpone
splash of milk (optional)

TO SERVE:
a handful of salted pistachios, roughly chopped
150 g (5½ oz) raspberries
mint springs

Melt the chocolate gently in a glass bowl over a saucepan of simmering water, stirring occasionally (the base of the bowl should not touch the water).

In a separate bowl, whip the cream to soft peaks. Whisk the lemon zest into the chocolate and then gently fold in the cream. Whisk in the mascarpone until smooth. If it starts looking grainy, add a splash of milk and continue mixing. Decant into a serving bowl.

Serve immediately or after chilling if preferred, scattered with chopped salted pistachios and raspberries, topped with extra lemon zest and a sprig of mint. You could also marinate the berries and currants in a little fresh lemon juice and sugar to make things a bit juicier.

Lemon Tiramisù

I may have resisted the temptation to call this 'lemonisu' (partly because it doesn't sound right anyway) but I could not resist writing a recipe for a pale yellow, lemony *tiramisù*. Of course, a real *tiramisù* should have coffee and cocoa (and in my mind, marsala and brandy), but this is a truly heavenly (if heathen) version, which, quite apart from being delicious, has a strong aesthetic argument behind it; such swathes of lemon yellow and pale cream seem like some sort of divinely luxurious sofa, smug and snug in the corner of an idyllic Amalfi residence.

If you happen to have any leftover lemon cake, such as the recipes on pages 132 or 135, use that as it will be even better. Some people like to soak the sponge layer in limoncello, but I find it both too sweet and too strong, so I have left it out. This version is innocent, unapologetically creamy and child-friendly.

FOR THE LEMON CURD:
2 teaspoons cornflour
  (cornstarch)
50 ml (1¾ fl oz/3½
  tablespoons) water
120 ml (4 fl oz/½ cup) lemon juice
3 eggs
150 g (5½ oz/¾ cup) sugar
40 g (1½ oz) unsalted butter
a pinch of salt

FOR THE CREAM:
400 g (14 oz/2 cups) mascarpone
300 ml (10 fl oz/1¼ cups)
  whipping cream
80 g (2¾ oz/½ cup plus
  1 tablespoon) icing
  (confectioner's) sugar

FOR THE SPONGE LAYER:
2 packs of savoiardi or
  ladyfingers (about 24 biscuits),
  or leftover cake
  (see introduction)
400 ml (14 fl oz/generous
  1½ cups) milk

TO FINISH:
lemon zest
lemon slices
sprigs of mint

First, make the curd. Whisk the cornflour with the water until dissolved and milky-looking, then place all the ingredients in a small saucepan over a low heat. Whisk constantly, helping the butter to melt, then gradually increase the heat to medium and stir until it thickens to form a curd the consistency of loose mayonnaise. Allow to cool to room temperature.

Whip the mascarpone with the cream and icing sugar to form soft peaks. Decant into a piping (pastry) bag if you have one.

Soak the savoiardi in milk, allowing them to absorb enough to become just damp and spongey but not dripping, then layer them at the base of a 23 cm (9 in) dish. Pipe over a third of the cream, flatten with a spatula or back of a spoon, then spread over half of the cooled curd. Repeat, then finish with little piped peaks of cream.

If you do not have a piping bag or prefer not to use one, you can layer differently and finish with a shining layer of yellow curd, which is equally beautiful. In this case, do two layers of both: start sponge, then cream, then curd; sponge, cream and finally curd. To finish, arrange the lemon zest, slices and sprigs of mint on top.

Fried Almond Ravioli

Raviolini di Mandorle

These tiny, fried almond ravioli are a traditional carnival sweet of Sardinia, and are wonderfully decorative and delicious. The pastry is melt-in-the-mouth, and the filling simple, sweet and spiked with plenty of lemon zest; it is easy to eat twenty without even thinking about it. The method is similar to savoury ravioli, but they are usually smaller and with much less filling, as a little goes a long way. The perfect thing for a *festa*, and further edible proof that not all fried things are heavy and fatty, but frequently dainty and delightful.

La pasta violata: This pastry is worth further explanation. *La pasta violata/violada* is the pastry that forms the base for the majority of Sardinian *dolci*. The word *violata* derives from the Sardinian word *violare* which has the same meaning as *ammorbidire* in Italian, or 'to make soft'. This in turn is derived from the Latin *figulare,* which means *ungere* in Italian, which in turn means 'soften a dough by impregnating it with fat', similar to the way we make flaky pastry or puff pastry.

The fat used is always *strutto*, which is lard. This gives the finished dough an inimitable flavour and texture (which I adore), but if you are vegetarian/vegan you can use butter or olive oil. The finished result is flaky, crisp, light and melting, and the traditional method of making the pastry by hand and gradually incorporating the fat renders a better, flakier result, as well as being enormously satisfying and leaving your hands moisturised.

If short of time, by all means throw everything in a mixer and let it do the work for you, but remember that a good bit of hand work can be very therapeutic.

250 g (8¾ oz/1¾ cups plus 2 tablespoons) semola rimacinato (or plain/all-purpose flour)
5 g (1 teaspoon) salt
120–130 ml (4–4½ fl oz/½ cup) tepid water
50 g (1¾ oz) lard (see introduction), at room temperature
sunflower or other neutral oil, for frying
icing (confectioner's) sugar, for dusting

FOR THE FILLING:
200 g (7 oz) blanched almonds, blitzed to a fine rubble (a little uneven is a good thing)
40 g (1½ oz) egg white (about 1 large egg white)
90 g (3¼ oz/½ cup) sugar
grated zest of 1 large lemon and a squeeze of the juice

First, make the dough. Combining the semola, salt and water in a bowl and work with your hands to form a shaggy dough, feeling as it comes together with no dry sandy bits (you may not need all the water). Tip out onto a clean work surface and knead vigorously until you have a smooth dough.

Once you have a smooth dough, roll it out flat and spread over around a quarter of the lard. Fold and knead until it is incorporated. It will seem a sticky mess for a bit, but keep at it. Repeat the process several times, adding the lard in four or five batches, then knead until you have a smooth and supple dough. Use in a day or so (store in the refrigerator if making in advance) or freeze.

To make the almond filling, mix all the ingredients together in a bowl and set aside.

Roll out the dough, using a pasta machine or rolling pin, into 10 cm (4 in) wide strips as thin as pasta for making ravioli, then place ½ teaspoons of almond mixture at 5 cm (2 in) intervals along the strips. Fold the dough over and close with

a pasta cutter as if making ravioli. You can make half-moon shapes or square as you prefer, and use cutters of your choice.

Bring a pan of oil to frying temperature (180°C/400°F, or until a cube of bread turns golden in 20 seconds) and fry in batches until just crisp and beginning to just turn golden at the edges. This will take a few minutes, and you may have to keep on turning them. Drain on paper towels, then dust with icing sugar and eat, hot or cold.

Lemon Custard Ravioli

Ravioli di Crema

It is nearly impossible not to fall in love with these deep-fried parcels of custard, which will be incredibly popular with children and anyone who is nostalgic about *crema* (custard), which must be nearly everyone. I fill these fuller than the almond ones on page 168 because the almond filling is intense and only a little is needed, whereas, as Lorenzo so rightly says, 'The custard is never enough.'

Use the same method as above but put dollops of thick lemon custard inside your ravioli before frying and dusting with icing (confectioner's) sugar.

500 ml (17 fl oz/2 cups) whole milk
zest of 2 lemons
130 g (4¾ oz/⅔ cup) sugar
60 g (2 oz/½ cup plus 1 tablespoon) cornflour (cornstarch)
6 egg yolks
1 x quantity pasta violata dough (see page 168)
sunflower or other neutral oil, for frying icing (confectioners') sugar, for dusting

Bring the milk to the boil in a saucepan with the lemon zest.

In a bowl, whisk the sugar and cornflour together with the egg yolks until smooth, then whisk in the hot milk. Return to the pan and cook over a low heat for about 10 minutes until thick, stirring continuously. Strain through a sieve (fine mesh strainer) to remove the zest (push through the mesh with a spoon), then chill completely before using.

Roll out the dough following the method on page 168, then fill with dessertspoons of the chilled custard. Fry following the method on page 168, then dust with icing sugar before serving.

Lemon Self-saucing Pudding

Often it's imperfection that we fall in love with. A nose that's too big, a lopsided grin, the little wispy tufts of hair at the top of an ear. As with lovers, so with dishes, and one of the things that made my mother's puddings so good when I was a child was that they were very far from perfect and she often slightly under (or over) cooked them.

Her most famous was Eve's pudding, which consisted of whatever sour fruit (gooseberries/rhubarb) she had grown that season, stewed and topped with a simple buttery sponge. Undercooking such sponge meant that the pudding's centre was deliciously gooey and provided a sort of creamy fruit sauce – hot, buttery, sweet and a perfect contrast to the fluffy crumb of the properly cooked parts. Once the pudding had been duly doused in cream, this warm and sticky sauce mixed with the cold cream to create something that was truly ambrosial.

Which brings me to self-saucing puddings. This pudding is pure nostalgia. Nostalgia must never be tinkered with, so I have kept it classic and traditional, it would be a crime to try to fancify this fresh-faced, fluffy and angelic nursery pudding. Almost a soufflé, almost a sponge, this pudding is truly a wonderful thing, quick to rustle up for hungry loved ones with a craving for something sweet. I can do the entire process with just two bowls and 20 minutes (I have often cooked it in the enamel bowl I mixed it in). Like those my mum made, it is cooked in the same dish as it is served in, a bonus for the washer-upper, and nicely unfussy. I often prefer a gratin dish on a table with scoops taken out of it, rather than fiddly individual portions.

60 g (2 oz) unsalted butter, plus extra for greasing
180 g (6¼ oz/1 cup minus 1½ tablespoons) caster (superfine) sugar
zest and juice of 2 large lemons
3 eggs, separated
60 g (2 oz/scant ½ cup) plain (all-purpose) or 00 flour
300 ml (10 fl oz/1¼ cups) whole milk
a good pinch of salt
cream, to serve

Preheat the oven to 160°C fan (180°C/350°F). Lightly butter a deep, ovenproof dish.

Cream the butter, sugar and lemon zest together until well combined. Beat in the egg yolks, one at a time, until incorporated. Fold in the flour and the milk until you have a smooth batter, then gradually mix in the lemon juice.

In a separate bowl whisk the egg whites with the salt until they form soft peaks and then carefully fold them into the cake batter.

Decant the mixture into the buttered dish and stand it in a roasting tin filled with water to come about halfway up the side of the dish.

Bake in the oven or 45–50 minutes until golden. Eat warm with cold cream.

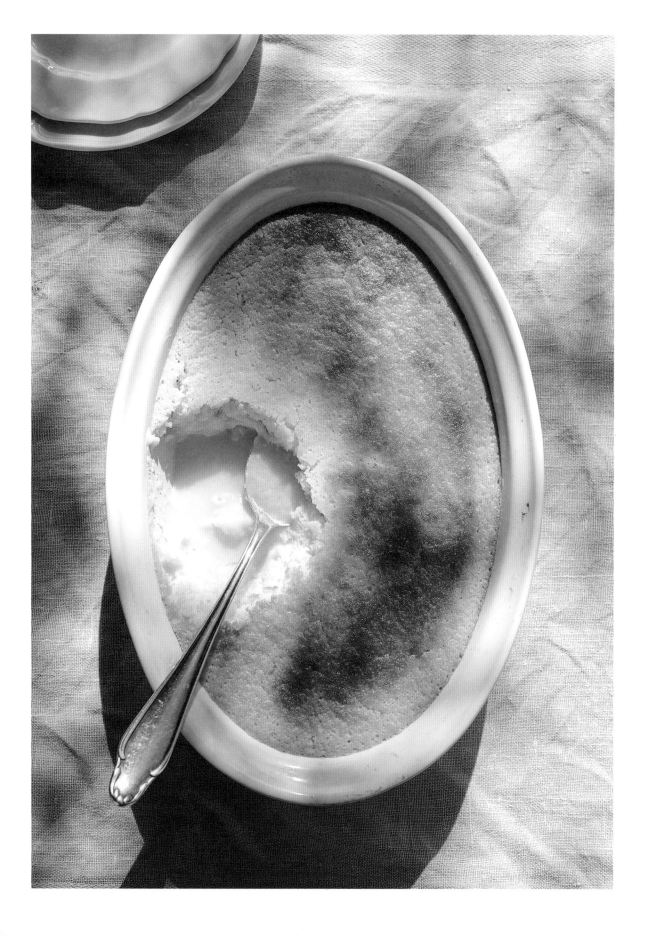

Sussex Pond Pudding

And so here it is, plump and proud and plain in this otherwise rather slick and chic Mediterranean volume, a bravely brown and inevitably buttery British pudding. Fluffy dumpling pastry, a pool of sweet, sharp and shining sauce, I need little persuasion to make this, but then, how could anyone resist a pudding with such a name? Its construction, too, is simplicity itself, somewhat reminiscent of building sandcastles on the beach, as a whole, cheerfully yellow lemon is buried in a bed of sandy brown sugar and butter, then topped with a soft, white, doughy pastry lid. It really does feel like child's play.

Sussex pond pudding is one of the best puddings I know, the pond referring to the sauce that floods from the pudding as it is cut into. This sauce, and the pudding itself, have a flavour that is reminiscent of buttered toast, toffee and marmalade.

Now, it does take a long time to cook, but I would advise doing it on a Sunday, and take advantage of a lit oven to bake some other bits in there too (a slow-roasted chicken and some vegetables, perhaps). The only fiddle is making its little pleated hat and tying it with string, which is a job I rather like.

I have replaced the traditional suet with butter to make it more user-friendly, but by all means go for suet if you have it. Grating butter is a surprisingly satisfactory activity.

180 g (6⅓ oz/1⅓ cups)
  plain (all-purpose) flour
a pinch of salt
1 teaspoon baking powder
90 g (3¼ oz) very cold unsalted
  butter, grated (you can use it
  from the freezer, if you wish,
  to stop it melting)
120 ml (4 fl oz/½ cup)
  whole milk
100 g (3½ oz) unsalted butter,
  plus extra
  for greasing
100 g (3½ oz/½ cup)
  demerara sugar
1 whole, unwaxed lemon
cream, to serve

Preheat the oven to 160°C fan (180°C/350°F) and fill a deep baking tray with hot water (this will become the bain-marie for your pudding). Grease a 750-ml (25-fl oz/3¼-cup) pudding basin generously with butter and line the base with a piece of greaseproof paper.

Mix the flour, salt, baking powder and grated butter together in a bowl and make a well in the centre. Pour in the milk and bring together to form a smooth dough (you may have a few drops of milk left). Wrap in a plastic bag and chill briefly.

Roll out two-thirds of the dough to line the pudding basin. Next, make the filling. Mix the sugar and butter together to form a rough, sandy mass. Place half of this mixture into the base of the lined pudding basin.

Cut three deep slits in the lemon, but not quite all the way through, so it stays intact. Place the lemon on the sugar-and-butter bed and then bury it like a coffin with the remaining mixture.

Roll out the remaining piece of dough. Wet the edges of the pastry and secure the lid, pressing it with your fingers to seal.

Cut out two pieces of greaseproof paper larger than the lid, and one piece of foil, and make a pleat in the middle of all of them, about 2.5 cm (1 in) thick. Secure all three layers (foil uppermost) on top of the basin with string (with some overhang) and form a string handle to help you lift it out later, like a little flower basket.

Place the pudding basin in the bain-marie, making sure the water comes at least two-thirds up the side of the basin, and cook for 3½ hours.

Remove from the oven, unmould onto a serving plate and serve with lashings of cold cream. I highly recommend it for breakfast the next morning too, warm or cold with a cup of coffee.

Lazy Lemon Meringue Pie

I wanted to include a lemon meringue pie because, in theory, it's spectacular: just the right amount of gauche, all wobbling yellow jelly curd, crumbling beige pastry and billowing white meringue curves, which form a glorious crunchy and fluffy hat. In practise, it's often saccharine, claggy and underwhelming. Like so many dishes that have become legends, it is all too easy to find mediocre versions. The LMP relies heavily on the perfect balance of texture and taste, and as far as I am concerned the trick to making a truly memorable one is to make the pastry almost entirely sugarless and the faintest bit nutty with some almonds, then the curd extremely tangy and the inevitably sweet meringue crisp and mallowy at the same time.

This is a minimum-faff version: the pastry can be pressed in as a 'crumb' without rolling, resting or chilling, and the curd is cooked all in one go (many versions involve stages). It can be knocked up in under an hour, no sweat.

FOR THE BASE:
120 g (4¼ oz/scant 1 cup) plain (all-purpose) or 00 flour
100 g (3½ oz) butter, plus extra for greasing
40 g (1½ oz/3¼ tablespoons) caster (superfine) sugar
40 g (1½ oz/½ cup) flaked (slivered) almonds
a good pinch of salt

FOR THE CURD:
30 g (1 oz/¼ cup plus 1 tablespoon) cornflour (cornstarch)
juice of 6 lemons plus grated zest of 2
70 ml (2½ fl oz/5 tablespoons) water
4 egg yolks
30 g (1 oz/2 tablespoons) butter, unsalted
good pinch of salt
200 g (7 oz/1 cup) sugar

FOR THE MERINGUE:
4 egg whites
2 teaspoons lemon juice
220 g (8 oz/1 cup plus 2 tablespoons) sugar

Preheat the oven to 150°C fan (170°C/340°F). Grease a 23 cm (9 in) pie dish.

Blitz the ingredients for the base together in a food processor until you have a fine crumb (or rub the butter in by hand as if making a crumble – the almonds will break up sufficiently between firm fingers). Using the back of a spoon, press the mixture over the base of the tin to form an even, flat layer. Bake in the oven for 20–25 minutes until golden. Remove and set aside to cool.

To make the curd, whisk the cornflour into the lemon juice and water, then combine with the remaining ingredients in a small saucepan over a medium heat. Cook, whisking constantly, until the thickness of custard. This will take longer than you think, but have faith, it will thicken eventually. Once thick, remove from the heat. Leave for a few minutes, then strain into a bowl and then allow to cool (I bung it in the freezer for a few minutes). Once cool, spread over the base (it needs to be cool otherwise the meringue will melt when you spread it on top).

Next, preheat increase the oven to 170°C fan (190°C/375°F). Make the meringue by whisking the egg whites with the lemon juice until they form stiff, glossy peaks, then whisk in the sugar a spoonful at a time until you have smooth peaks again. Swoosh the meringue over the curd, making peaks with a fork, and then bake in the oven for 15–20 minutes until just coloured on top.

Serve cold or at room temperature.

Pavlova with Lemon-olive Oil Curd

A perfect late spring/early summer pudding, which plays on quintessential Italian flavours. Unlike the traditional (and often overly sweet) pavlova, I prefer a tangy yoghurt cream and velvety curd with just the slight background note of olive oil, which chimes beautifully with the fragrant basil.

Decorate with your favourite edible flowers (such as jasmine) and strawberries, or your favourite summer berries. I make double my usual pavlova recipe as it deserves to be mighty and magnificent for a *festa*, but if you are making for a smaller more subdued setting, by all means halve the recipe.

FOR THE PAVLOVA:
6 egg whites
350 g (12 oz/1¾ cups) sugar
zest of 3 lemons plus
    1 tablespoon juice
10 g (2 teaspoons) cornflour
    (cornstarch)

FOR THE YOGHURT CREAM:
250 ml (8 fl oz/1 cup) double
    (heavy) cream
200 g (7 fl oz/scant 1 cup)
    Greek yoghurt
3 tablespoons icing
    (confectioner's) sugar

FOR THE LEMON-OLIVE OIL CURD:
5 g (1 scant tablespoon)
    cornflour (cornstarch)
juice of 2 lemons
1 egg plus 2 egg yolks
140 g (5¼ oz/⅔ cup) sugar
40 g (1½ oz) butter
30 ml (2 tablespoons) extra
    virgin olive oil
a pinch of salt

TO FINISH (OPTIONAL):
200 g (7 oz) strawberries,
    halved
edible flowers
basil leaves
lemon zest squiggles

Preheat the oven to 130°C fan (150°C/300°F). Line a baking tray with baking parchment.

Whisk the egg whites with the lemon juice until they form stiff, satin-like peaks. Add the sugar a spoonful at a time, whisking all the time. Once all of the sugar has been incorporated and the meringue is once again in stiff and silky peaks, whisk in the lemon zest and cornflour.

Spread the meringue out into a large circle on the lined baking tray, making the edges a little higher than the middle to allow for the filling (I aim for pizza size, i.e. about 25 cm/10 in). Bake in the oven for around 1 hour until crisp (gently check the underside), then turn off the oven, open the door and leave to cool completely before topping.

To make the yoghurt cream, whip the cream in a bowl until you have soft peaks, then stir in the yoghurt and icing sugar.

To make the curd, whisk the cornflour into the lemon juice until dissolved, then pour into a small saucepan, add all the remaining ingredients and place over a medium-low heat. This will take around 10 minutes. Cook, whisking continuously, until it becomes thick and velvety. Set aside to cool until ready to use.

To finish, spread the cream over the top of the pavlova and then dot over the curd. Scatter over edible flowers, strawberries, basil leaves and lemon zest squiggles to your liking, and serve.

Almond, Pistachio & Lemon Gelato

Three of my favourite things in a gelato, with a zingy, slightly salty and nutty flavour. The two different nuts both contribute to the overall flavour, and as is so often the case in many of my nut recipes, almonds do the leg work while the richer, sweeter and more capricious pistachio flutters in for a final lift of flavour. Try as an affogato, proving that lemon and coffee always go together.

100 g (3½ oz) shelled pistachios
80 g (2¾ oz) whole blanched
  almonds
4 egg yolks
220 g (8 oz/1 cup plus
  2 tablespoons) sugar
240 ml (8 fl oz/1 cup) whole
  milk
480 ml (17 fl oz/2 cups) double
  (heavy) cream
a pinch of salt
zest and juice of 1 small lemon
crushed pistachios, to serve
whipped cream, to serve

Preheat the oven to 150°C fan (170°C/340°F).

Place the nuts on a baking sheet and roast in the oven for about 12 minutes, until just turning golden. Remove from the oven and chop or blitz to a rubble.

Mix the egg yolks with the sugar in a heatproof bowl and whisk well. Meanwhile warm the milk with the cream in a saucepan over a medium heat until at a scald. Pour the milk mixture into the egg yolks in a steady stream, whisking all the time, then return the mixture to the pan and cook over a low heat, stirring continuously, until it has thickened and just coats the back of a wooden spoon (it will be coming to a rolling boil at this point).

Remove from the heat, pour into a bowl and stir in the toasted chopped nuts, salt and lemon zest and juice. Chill in the refrigerator overnight for the flavours to develop.

The next day, strain out the nuts and churn in an ice-cream maker according to the manufacturer's. If you like, you can serve with some crushed pistachios and freshly whipped cream (just to gild the lily).

Note: The remaining nuts can be eaten on breakfast muesli/granola.

Lemon & Wild Fennel Sorbetto

All the soft, sweet herbs, such as chervil, basil, mint, tarragon and wild fennel which grows like a weed in many parts of Italy (particularly Sardinia), work brilliantly in sweets. Lemon is such an agreeable and adaptable partner to almost any flavour; here it highlights the citrus notes in the fennel. This combination crops up in several recipes in the book and is one of my favourites. Decorated with a little feathery frond, this is elegant to look at, the palest lemon-green colour, and wonderfully refreshing to eat. It works particularly well in high summer after a lunch of garlicky seafood pasta or baked fish.

If you wish to serve this in frosted lemons on glass dishes, it has extra charm.

6 lemons (if you wish to serve
  the sorbet in them, optional)
zest of 2 lemons
300 ml (10 fl oz/1¼ cups) water
280 g (9¾ oz/1½ cups minus
  2 tablespoons) sugar
4–5 fronds of wild fennel
  (or basil or mint leaves)
250 ml (8 fl oz/1 cup) lemon
  juice

**FOR THE FROSTED
LEMONS (OPTIONAL):**
6–8 lemons

If you wish to serve this in lemons, cut off the lower 1 cm (½ in) of the fruit to create a flat base. Cut the tops off for the hats, scoop out the flesh and press it to make your juice. Freeze the shells so they look extra frosty and inviting.

To make the sorbet, combine the lemon zest, water and sugar in a saucepan. Bring to the boil and simmer for 3–5 minutes until syrupy. Once tepid, add the herbs, blitz and then strain, then reduce the heat and add the lemon juice. Churn according to your ice cream machine's instructions and serve in the hollowed-out lemons, if you wish.

Melon, Lemon & Basil Sorbet

The delicate, almost ethereal sweetness of melon works beautifully when sharpened by plentiful fresh lemon juice and enhanced by fragrant basil. Playing on the peppery basil of this sorbet, I like to serve it with a drizzle of my most fragrant olive oil. It's Mediterranean summer in a mouthful.

200 ml (7 fl oz/scant 1 cup) water
150 g (5½ oz/¾ cup) sugar
a few basil leaves, torn, plus extra to serve
1 medium melon (I like Cantaloupe)
juice of 4 lemons
a little extra virgin olive oil, to serve

Combine the water and sugar in a saucepan and bring to the boil, then reduce the heat and simmer for a few minutes until you have a simple sugar syrup. Remove from the heat and leave to cool. Add the torn basil leaves, stir and leave to infuse at room temperature for at least 20 minutes.

Cut the melon into chunks, remove the peel and discard the seeds. Blitz the melon flesh with the syrup and then strain through a sieve (fine-mesh strainer). Add the lemon juice, tasting as you go to check the sweetness.

Churn in an ice-cream maker according to the manufacturer's instructions or freeze in a shallow tray as a granita, raking it with a fork every so often as it freezes. Serve decorated with a few basil leaves.

Lemon, Pear & Lemon Verbena Sorbet

This is another favourite sorbet, which I included in my second book, but perhaps because it had no accompanying photo, I feel it didn't get the recognition it deserved. Lemon verbena has a wonderful, sherbety flavour, and brings out the best in the unapologetically sweet but somewhat subtle pears.

150 g (5½ oz/¾ cup) sugar
280 ml (9 fl oz/1 cup plus
  2 tablespoons) water
6–7 good ripe pears
  (around 800 g/1 lb 12 oz)
8–9 fresh lemon verbena
  leaves
juice of 2 large lemons

Make a syrup by placing the sugar and water in a saucepan, bringing to a gentle simmer (swirling the pan from time to time) and leaving for a minute or two until shiny and clear.

Peel the pears and core them, then cut into rough pieces (if they begin to go brown, squeeze over some lemon juice). Drop them immediately into the syrup and cover with a piece of baking parchment (this prevents them from discolouring). Poach over a gentle heat for 2–3 minutes. Remove from the heat and add half the lemon verbena leaves. Leave to infuse at room temperature for at least 15 minutes.

Remove the lemon verbena leaves and discard them. Blitz the pears and their syrup along with the lemon juice and the fresh verbena leaves until you have a pulp.

Strain through a sieve (fine-mesh strainer), then churn in an ice-cream maker according to the manufacturer's instructions. Decant into a sealable container and cover. Freeze until ready to serve, then remove from the freezer a few minutes before serving.

Lemon Flowers

Orange blossom, or the flowers from the bitter orange tree, are well known in the kitchen, mostly in the form of orange blossom water. Lemon flowers are also edible, as are all the blossoms of the citrus family. Lemon blossoms have a similar scent to their better-known orange counterparts, which manages to be both strong and delicate, and I would be hard pressed to distinguish them in a blind sniff test. They add a wonderful fragrance and flavour to sweets.

One of my favourite ways of using them is marinating them with some fresh fruit and extra lemon juice, which adds an ethereal, almost candy-like flavour to the fruit. Try it with fresh strawberries (the seasons coincide here in Sardinia; the lemon is in full bloom just as the first strawberries arrive) or sliced blood oranges.

The other way I have eaten them, which I have never been brave enough to reproduce, is candied as a Greek spoon sweet. The candied lemon blossoms, tiny curls of translucent and palest gold, were set upon a bed of thick, lily-white Greek yoghurt, to be eaten by the spoonful, served just before coffee. It is one of the most delicious and magical things I have ever eaten. Perhaps one day, when my own lemon tree produces flowers in abundance, I will attempt to make my own.

A Squeeze of Lemon

Four

Rosemary, Lemon & Anchovy Butter

An incredibly useful and addictive butter to have up your sleeve, this is delicious melted onto all sorts of things, from pork chops to eggs to broccoli. Accessorise as you see fit with a pinch of chilli (hot pepper) flakes, a dash of paprika, etc.

6–8 anchovy fillets
zest and juice of ½ lemon
1 garlic clove
100 g (3½ oz) unsalted butter
1 tablespoon chopped
  rosemary

Blitz all the ingredients together in a food processor until smooth, then chill until ready to use. Slather on to hot eggs/toast/meat/vegetables.

Lemony Tahini Dressing

Tahini is a sesame seed paste that comes in dark or light varieties and varies hugely in quality, but any will work for this recipe. Tahini has the same ability as nut butters to be creamy, but offers an infinitely deeper flavour profile. I miss using this magic substance on a regular basis, as it is not easily found in Sardinia.

To my mind, this recipe is even better than hummus (hummus being the recipe tahini is most known for) and is incredibly versatile. We serve it with grilled mackerel (it works best with meaty fish), roasted aubergines (eggplant), grilled lamb, fried courgettes (zucchini), flatbreads, spiced tagines, roasted vegetables, salads, falafel... it goes with just about anything. Sometimes I like to swirl a fat dollop of thick Greek yoghurt through it, which makes it extra creamy.

1 small garlic clove
1 teaspoon sea salt, or to taste
200 g (7 oz/1 cup minus
  2 tablespoons) tahini
juice of 1½ large or 2 small
  lemons
30 ml (2 tablespoons) extra
  virgin olive oil, plus extra
  for drizzling
90 ml (3 fl oz/⅓ cup) water

TO FINISH (OPTIONAL):
chopped sweet herbs (such as
  mint, dill or parsley)
a dollop of Greek yoghurt
dried chilli (hot pepper) flakes
  or smoked paprika

Chop the garlic into small pieces, then press and grind it with the salt using the flat side of a knife (or use a press if you prefer). Put it into a bowl with the tahini and lemon juice and whisk. At this point, things will get ugly and the tahini will begin to look grainy and split. Plough on regardless.

Whisk in the oil (things will look even weirder at this point, but don't worry). Now whisk in the water until you have a smooth, creamy, pale beige sauce. Taste for seasoning, adding a pinch more salt if necessary. Use immediately, garnish with any of the optional extras, or keep in the refrigerator for up to a week.

Variation: Very Lemony Green Tahini Sauce

Follow the instructions for the sauce above, adding a handful of mint, parsley and dill at the end and then blitz to a smooth consistency.

Lemony Fennel & Potato Purée

An excellent side dish for baked fish, squid, braised octopus, roast chicken, meatballs or pork, this is a simple but effective combination the colour of a pale December day, but with a distinctive Mediterranean flavour. It sits prettily, subtly and silkily beneath all sorts of salty grilled/braised things. I first ate it under some spicy tomato-braised octopus, and it worked beautifully. Use your very best olive oil, it will make all the difference.

Serve with some grilled or roasted fish, squid or prawns (shrimp), lemon-marinated peppers and lemon zest salsa verde. Also very good with any dish containing olives (which bring out the olive oil beautifully).

1 fennel bulb (about 300 g/10½ oz), tough outer bits removed
300 g (10½ oz, or 3 largish) waxy potatoes, peeled
salt
4–5 tablespoons extra virgin olive oil
zest and juice of ½ large lemon

Cut the fennel and potatoes into roughly equal pieces and place them in saucepan. Just cover them with water and add a generous pinch of salt. Bring to a simmer and cook for about 10 minutes until tender. Drain.

Transfer the fennel and potatoes to a food processor and blitz until smooth, then add in the oil, lemon zest and juice and salt to taste. It should be sweet but peppy, with a rich, peppery undertone from the oil. Use warm (this can easily be made in advance and reheated).

Note: If you have any left, add a splash of milk or cream and a little stock if you have it (a cube and some water are also fine) for the most deliciously creamy and silky soup.

Lemon IN THE KITCHEN

In my own kitchen, lemon is my most-used seasoning, second only to salt. Without lemons, olive oil and salt, I simply couldn't cook. Lemons appear in our kitchens all year around, unfazed by the constantly shifting culinary landscape. Everybody uses lemon, it is a unifying seasoning, irrespective of geography or budget.

A bowl of lemons on the table is a soothing sight, but it is also an invitation and an opportunity. Having fresh lemons to hand means being able to truly change the flavour of our food. One of the hardest things about writing this book was choosing the recipes that merited inclusion, when realistically almost every dish I have ever made could have made a case for squeezing itself between these pages. There are, after all, so very few dishes that are not improved by a lemon in some way or another.

It is not just my own or the more general Sardinian kitchen that has come to rely on lemons in this way. As Elizabeth David notes in her essay 'I'll Be With You in the Squeezing of a Lemon': 'During the past four hundred years the lemon has become, in cooking, the condiment which has largely replaced the vinegar, the verjuice, the pomegranate juice, the bitter orange juice, the mustard and wine compounds which were the acidifiers poured so freely into the cooking pots of sixteenth- and seventeenth-century Europe. There are indeed times when a lemon as seasoning seems second only in importance to salt'. In Mediterranean cooking specifically, David writes, 'Lemon juice is the astringent corrective, as well as the flavouring, for olive-oil-based dishes and fat meat'. The natural counterpart to many a dish, sauce or piece of meat that contains or is seasoned with olive oil is a squeeze of lemon juice. The final addition of a drizzle of flavoursome olive oil and a squeeze of fresh lemon is what elevates and finishes innumerable dishes.

A seasoning is defined as something which 'enhances, improves or elevates' other food. In most dictionary definitions of seasonings, it is likely you will find salts and spices, rather than lemon juice, but lemon juice has similar transformative seasoning properties. Lemon can elevate, enhance and improve the flavour of almost anything it is added to, but rather than simply making food taste more strongly of itself, as salt does, it also acts as a corrective, providing contrast, balance and harmony. A squeeze of lemon on ripe fruit can enhance said fruit's flavour, making it more vivid and lively, while correcting the acidity levels of a plate of earthy chickpeas is a perfect example of the essential and infinitely pleasurable contrast lemon juice can provide.

Lemon juice and its innate astringency are thus both the corrective and enhancer in so many dishes, serving to cut, balance, temper, enliven, brighten, lift and freshen. Lemon, like the perfect lover, brings out the best in whatever it is paired with.

Zesty Salsa Verde

There are many versions of this delicious green sauce, but this is mine, which tastes like falling face-first into a particularly bushy herb patch. The lemon lifts and accentuates the fresh, citrussy notes of all of these inherently sweet herbs.

The original salsa verde, according to the great and authoritative food writer Gillian Riley, included breadcrumbs soaked in lemon juice and also hard-boiled eggs and garlic. I leave the garlic as a whisper rather than a shout, as the freshness of herbs and lemon are the flavours I want to sing here. A little red wine vinegar is, for me, necessary to remonstrate with the salt of the anchovies, and the lemon juice is there to lift everything. It's a sauce which, when made well, perfectly demonstrates the essential balance that is at the heart of good cooking, and specifically good sauce making.

I advise you to chop or pound by hand, for it is impossible not to feel your spirits lift when making (and smelling) this green tincture; the scent is pure aromatherapy. In practical rather than purely olfactory terms, hand-chopping means the herbs are less bruised, the sauce remains greener, and you will achieve what Gillian calls 'a tastier result with more personality'. I leave out mustard (which is sometimes added) and use my very best olive oil to give extra punch.

Enjoy it dolloped alongside meat, fish, eggs or on top of bruschetta, beans, soup, potatoes and pulses. A truly wonderful, versatile, uplifting thing. It is difficult to give precise measurements for such an imprecise sauce, but when I say bunch of herbs, I mean the sort of bunch you can hold in your hand like a bouquet.

a bunch each of basil, mint
  and parsley
1 tablespoon capers
½ garlic clove
5 anchovy fillets
zest of 1 lemon and some
  of its juice
salt
extra virgin olive oil
a splash or two of red wine
  vinegar

Finely chop all of the ingredients by hand and mix with oil and vinegar to get a just dollop-able consistency. Taste for seasoning and add salt, lemon or more oil as you see fit. (You can, of course, use a blender – it will still be delicious.)

Gremolata

The more spartan sister of salsa verde (page 204), gremolata is a wonderful, versatile and pretty thing that can be used to especially good effect when sprinkled on top of very rich meat braises before serving (such as the traditional *osso buco*), but also works well with braised fish or octopus (it is also good on salt cod). It is more than just the decorative 'parsley dust' that my grandmother insisted on sprinkling on everything, as the savoury hit of zingy lemon means it genuinely contributes to the finished dish. An extremely useful thing to have in your culinary repertoire.

a bunch of parsley
zest of ½ lemon
1 small garlic clove

Chop everything together to a fine green crumb and then use immediately.

Preserved Lemon & Herb Yoghurt Dressing

When I worked at the lovely restaurant Spring in London we used to make a version of this often, mostly to go with sea bass, but I have since made many variants of it to go with just about anything. It is palest green and herb-flecked, and wonderfully fresh due to the inclusion of both preserved lemons and fresh ones. A very versatile thing to make for barbecues, grilled vegetables, or to have as a salad dressing or for dunking bread into.

½ garlic clove
1 tablespoon Cheat's Preserved
  Lemons (page 232), mostly
  rind pieces
zest and juice of 1 large lemon
150 g (5 fl oz/scant ⅔ cup)
  thick plain yoghurt
1 teaspoon runny honey
a handful of mint leaves
a handful of dill or wild fennel
  fronds
a handful of parsley leaves
4–5 tablespoons extra virgin
  olive oil
sea salt

Place all of the ingredients in a food processor and blitz until the herbs are just pale green flecks and you have a runny, creamy sauce. I particularly like this with roasted red vegetables or grilled peppers.

Lemon JUICE IN SALADS

I use a range of different vinegars, which I love and value for their individual and diverse flavours. However, lemon juice has a fresh, clean acidity that is superior to any vinegar exactly because of its 'cleanness' – a clumsy term to describe something almost indescribable.

Vinegar comes from wine (or cider or alcohol) and this fact means that it often has a complex and somewhat heavy flavour (there are notes of oak barrels, of red fruits in red wine vinegar, of sour apples in cider vinegar, etc). Lemon juice is not a by-product, has no murky or mixed flavour, and its purity means that in cooking it sings a clear soprano top note unweighted by any other aromatic clutter.

I often use lemon juice alongside vinegar to give extra freshness to salads and dressings; both contribute acidity in different but equally valid ways. The mixture of red wine vinegar (for fruity depth and punch) and lemon juice (for freshness and clarity) provides the balanced acidity for my most-often made mayonnaise, a perfect anchovy dressing for bitter greens, salsa verde and almost any sauce made with a peppery olive oil.

In raw vegetable salads, lemon juice can save aesthetics as well as acidity, as so many vegetables and fruits oxidise once cut and exposed to air. A fennel salad made with red wine vinegar would be anathema, partly because the muddy rose colour would taint the pale perfection of the sliced fennel, and partly because the vinegar's robust depth would ruin the delicacy of the wonderful, sweet and ethereal vegetable. If pushed to choose only one acidity for any salad, it would be lemon juice because it is so versatile and simultaneously sharp and subtle. It changes neither colour nor flavour, and like the other fundamental seasoning (salt) neither bullies, disguises or muddies, rather enhances, elevates and lifts the flavours that are already there. Its astringency has the ability to cut through fat like a knife slicing through warm butter. Vinegar, wonderful and essential ingredient though it is, cannot compete with its purity.

Lemon Drops

five

Lavender & Honey Lemonade

Elvio is an old friend of my father-in-law, Mauro, a fellow appreciator/maker of Vernaccia and the owner of the only lavender farm in Sardinia. Like the majority of Sardinians, the seemingly ageless Elvio was not content to pass a sedentary retirement and so hatched the plan of planting his land with lavender. The idea came to him after he visited Provence and saw the infamous lavender fields there. Luckily, the soil and conditions were right, and he created a beautiful and unique space just down the road from where we live. It has become popular with tourists and locals alike, and a favourite spot for wedding photography and the inevitable Instagram selfie. Under a shady canopy, Elvio, dressed in his scruffy straw hat, feeds you with his wife's homemade lavender shortbread and an iced lavender, lemon and honey tisane, his contagious, schoolboy grin fixed throughout as he recounts the story of his love for lavender.

This lemonade is a tribute to him, and something wonderfully refreshing to drink in the hottest months (you can also drink this hot in winter). The elixir of Elvio's eternal youth, and now perhaps yours, too.

juice of ½ lemon and a strip
  of zest
1–2 tablespoons honey
a few single buds of lavender
  (not the whole flower heads,
  the tiny buds are strong and
  a little goes a long way)

TO SERVE:
ice
lemon slices
lavender sprigs

Warm the water in a saucepan over a medium-low heat with the lemon zest and honey, stirring until melted. Add the lemon juice and the lavender buds and stir. Taste for seasoning, adding more honey, lemon or lavender according to preference. Leave to cool and infuse, then strain and serve over ice with a slice and a sprig. Dainty, refreshing and simple.

Espresso with Lemon

Back in my days as a pastry chef, one of the desserts I dreamt up was based around coffee and lemons; a warm, dark chocolate mousse served with creamy, cold lemon ice cream, whipped cream and espresso powder. Coffee – like proper, dark, high-cocoa chocolate – has inherent citrus notes, and thus pairs beautifully with lemon. One of my favourite chocolate bars is a dark 70 per cent cocoa solids chocolate studded with candied Amalfi lemon chunks. I like to dunk squares of it in my coffee.

The dark, rich, roasted and smoky notes of both coffee and dark chocolate are cut through beautifully by the fresh fragrance of lemon zest (it is important to remember that this match is with the aromatic zest rather than the astringent juice).

On the Amalfi Coast, and for many true Amalfitani, morning espresso is infused with a little lemon zest (and sometimes a little sugar too). It's a happy combination, and one I like to repeat when I have good fresh lemons to hand. I also recommend it as an iced coffee combination. It's wonderfully refreshing and uplifting.

Note: this is a flavour combination you can easily recreate when you drink a black coffee and eat a slice of lemon cake for breakfast (there is no shortage of breakfast lemon cakes/pudding recipes in this book for you to try).

espresso (or mocha) coffee
a little strip of fresh lemon peel
a shake of sugar or drizzle of
    honey (optional)

Make your coffee and place in your favourite cup. Add a strip of freshly peeled lemon zest and the sugar/honey if using. Inhale first, and then sip. Or, as explained on page 18, add the lemon to the top of your mocha pot.

Lemon
AID

Medicine & Miracle Cures

One of my most prized possessions is an early 18th-century recipe book written by one of my ancestors and given to me by my grandmother. In it you will find recipes such as 'a Good Way with Goose' and then on the adjacent page, 'To Cure a Cough'.

The first recipe books also contained cures for all sorts of ills, as food and cookery were not just a leisurely pursuit or pleasure, but also fundamental for true nourishment, in the more nutritional sense of the word. Thus, these early books were full of such semi-potions to cure a common cold and soothe a sore throat as well as silence a growling stomach.

This aspect of cookery and its power to cure is something I still keep in mind when writing recipes, and seems nowhere more appropriate than in a book about lemons, the original miracle fruit that has both the power to cure sickness and create delicious food.

LITTLE CATHEDRALS: WHAT'S IN A LEMON

Lemons are made up of the four P's: peel, pith, pulp and pips. The peel contains oil glands, which open via pores in the surface – what we see as a lemon's demure dimples – and this is why, when a lemon's skin is scratched by a sharp nail or sliced with a sharp knife, these oils are released and we smell the wonderful scent. Limonene, the main component of the lemon oil found in a lemon's peel, is used in cosmetics and cleaning products, and is what gives lemon oil its distinctive smell. It is antibacterial, antiviral and antifungal and also a natural solvent. In terms of its scent, it is said to be sedative and soothing, to lift the spirits and improve concentration. When researching this book I bought a small vial of pure lemon oil, which I kept by my desk, and took frequent, deep and slow sniffs from. I can testify that it does, indeed, lift the spirits and somehow sharpen the senses – it is the most alive scent that I know.

The pith is made up mostly of fibre and contains some antioxidants, while the pulp contains 90 per cent of a lemon's vitamin C content, and the pips contain large amounts of pectin. Pectin is a form of fibre and also a natural setting agent, which is useful in the kitchen: you will notice your lemon *marmellata* sets easily to a stiff gel. This is why lemon (often a whole lemon) is so often added to jams, as it will help the jam set.

Aside from the more expected beneficial effects, there are those that come as a surprise. In the late 1800s, Mediterranean women would use sea sponges soaked in lemon juice as a natural contraceptive. It is rumoured that Casanova urged his lovers to use a hollowed-out lemon half as a rudimentary diaphragm. This is less unscientific than you might think, as lemon juice can act as a natural spermicide.

Lemons are full of health-promoting components, such as antiseptics, antivirals, antifungals, antioxidants, anti-inflammatories and antihistamines. Lemon oil and its uplifting scent is said to be a natural antidepressant (I highly recommend taking a good daily whiff to boost a flat mood). However, the lemon's most notable and well-known health benefit is its vitamin C content.

In Italian, I was delighted to discover the adjective *scorbutico*, which means grumpy or irritable, and derives from the same root as the name for scurvy, or *scorbuto* as it is in Italian. Scurvy is a sickness that afflicted sailors for three centuries and killed over two million of them before a real cure was found, this cure being the seemingly innocuous ascorbic acid, or what is more commonly known as vitamin C. Scurvy was first recorded in the 15th century, when it broke out in Vasco da Gama's crew as he sailed around the Cape of Good Hope, but it was not until 1747 that a doctor named James Lind conducted a proper medical trial to show the effects of treating scurvy with lemon juice. Even after he proved its undeniably beneficial effects, the British Admiralty took more than 40 years to implement it into sailors' diets, when they were ordered to consume lemon juice mixed with sugar after two weeks at sea.

Scurvy is a disease with horrendous symptoms (bleeding gums, chronic fatigue, bruising and acute muscular pain) that affects the production of collagen, a vital connective tissue in the body. Humans, along with various other mammals including guinea pigs and monkeys, do not produce their own vitamin C (or ascorbic acid) and so must ingest it, mostly in fresh fruits and vegetables. A diet lacking in vitamin C – the diet for those at sea for extended periods of time, for example – would lead to scurvy and ultimately death. Lemons thus became an essential part of preserving the life of sailors and facilitating expeditions at sea. The cultivation of these large quantities of lemons to treat scurvy was a driving factor in Italy's lemon boom.

While scurvy is not likely to affect many of us, not being at sea and deprived of fresh vegetables and fruit for weeks on end, it is extraordinary to think of this vital element of citrus, of its life-giving properties, and its power to both heal the body and the mind.

A LEMON A DAY. . .

Drinking a glass of lemon water every day is similarly maintained to be beneficial, aiding digestion, providing a daily dose of vitamin C and boosting skin health. The acid in the lemon promotes gastric acid production in the stomach, meaning food is broken down more easily. It is also a zingy way to wake up, if you drink it first thing in the morning, and to cleanse a dull and drowsy overnight palate, giving it a sharp wake up and paving the way for sweeter and more soothing things to follow. Ideally, after your juicy lemon water, you can then sip a coffee aromatic with a little zest (page 218).

Rose & Raspberry Lemonade

SERVES 2

Roses and raspberries are not just alliteratively suited, but in terms of flavour complement each other brilliantly; the floral and romantic rose cut through by sharp scarlet berry. Reminiscent of my granny's garden and an English summer – with some help from a holidaying Mediterranean lemon – this makes a wonderfully pink and refreshing drink perfect for high summer, and impossibly pretty to look at. Serve in or near a rose bush for full effect.

A good lemonade is a very good thing, but so is adding your favourite berry/herb combinations to it (try fresh pear juice and lemon verbena, or strawberries and tarragon).

80 g (2¾ oz/⅔ cup)
  raspberries, crushed
320 ml (11 fl oz/1¼ cups)
zest and juice of 2 lemons
2–3 tablespoons sugar
1½ tablespoons rose water

TO SERVE:
ice
fresh lemon slices
fresh rose petals/edible flowers
sprig of mint

Crush the raspberries roughly (or blitz if you like).

Combine the water, lemon zest and sugar in a small saucepan over a low heat. Heat for a few minutes to dissolve the sugar and extract the flavour from the zest, then set aside and allow to cool.

Once cool, add the crushed berries, rose water and lemon juice and taste. Adjust the sweetness/rose flavour accordingly, and then strain or serve as is over ice, decorated with lemon slices, edible flowers and/or a sprig of mint.

Amaretto Sour

For a short time in his chequered career my older brother was a cocktail waiter, and this was the drink he always made for me. The amaretto sour remains lodged in my affections, partly perhaps because it is so simple to make, and partly because it is the drinkable facsimile of one of my favourite biscuits (amaretti, page 120, which uses almost exactly the same ingredients). I am also a sucker for its retro aesthetics. It is the frothy personification of the quintessential glamorous Italian *signora*; the crowning maraschino cherry her red lipstick, the pale brown amaretto liqueur her signature camel coat. Flavour-wise too, there is something irresistible about it – the sour almond/cherry mix like an American cherry pie/Italian sour cherry pastry of your dreams, the lip-smacking lemon cutting through the sweetness, the creamy crowning froth that leaves just the shadow of a moustache on an upper lip.

For a short period when we were children, my mother went through a mid-life crisis that manifested itself mainly in her mixing herself a snowball at 6 o'clock every evening, sitting on the dog-eared old green velvet armchair in front of the TV and watching *Dirty Dancing*. When my mid-life crisis arrives, I would like my drink to be this. The film I have not yet decided.

The amaretto sour is an Italian American brainchild that was born in the 1970s, when a clever bartender who remains unknown decided to supplement the whisky in a classic sour with amaretto. The intensely sweet and fragrant almond flavour is cut through by plentiful fresh lemon juice, and then given a creamy froth by egg white. If you are vegan or don't like the idea of raw egg, use a tablespoon of aquafaba (chickpea/garbanzo water) or simply leave it out and add extra ice.

You ideally need a cocktail shaker.

60 ml (2 fl oz/¼ cup) amaretto
30 ml (2 tablespoons) lemon
 juice
1 teaspoon maraschino cherry
 syrup
1 teaspoon egg white

TO GARNISH:
maraschino cherry
lemon wedge
ice

Combine all the ingredients in a cocktail shaker, then serve in your favourite squat glass over ice. Garnish with a cherry and lemon wedge.

Lemon Jars

six

Proper Preserved Lemons

Traditionally used in Northern African (specifically Moroccan) cooking, preserved lemons are simply lemons that are salted and preserved using lemon juice and nothing else. Often referred to as pickled lemons, they are a canny way of storing lemons during the months when they are in abundance, ready and waiting for the months when they aren't, just like many other preserves. Because they are effectively 'cured' or almost cooked by the combination of salt and lemon juice (which preserves them), they have a sort of salted-marmalade, cooked flavour that is very different to fresh lemons, and which adds its own distinctive magic to many dishes.

HOW TO MAKE THEM

You will need clean, sterilised jars (page 234), a bag of sea salt and lots of lemons.

To sterilise jars, place them in a pan of boiling water for a few minutes. Cut each lemon into four wedges but do not cut all the way down, so the lemon opens like a four-petalled flower but stays intact. Stuff salt between the quarters and then press the lemons into a large jar. Continue with more lemons in the same manner until the jar is full, squashing them in tightly. Now squeeze some fresh lemon juice and pour it in until they are totally submerged. Place the lid on the jar and store in a cool, dark place for 3 weeks. Your lemons are now ready to use.

HOW TO USE THEM

The zest/skin is the most prized part, but the pulp is also usable. Both can be rinsed before draining if you are worried about saltiness. I do not add salt to the dish and don't necessarily rinse mine, depending on what I am making, so taste and then decide. The pulp needs to be strained through a sieve to remove the pips.

WHAT TO DO WITH THEM

Once ready, you can do all sorts of things with your preserved lemons. Once the jar is open, they keep for up to a year in the refrigerator, so even if you do not use them on a weekly basis it's still worth making a batch. Preserved lemons often only get used for tagines (for which they are perfect), but there are numerous ways in which you can use them – see opposite.

- Use them in dressings and vinaigrettes instead of or with fresh lemon (both zest and pulp)
- Bake them into shortbread biscuits (cookies) (don't add any salt to your dough)
- Blitz them into an ice cream (only a little, and again don't add salt to your base)
- Top labneh or fresh goat's cheese with some sliced rind
- Blitz into pesto (pulp or rind or both)
- Add to an aïoli (either pulp or rind or both)
- Add to cocktails or sodas
- Toss sliced rind through a sweet roasted vegetable salad (such as roasted carrots) and add soft cheese to finish
- As above but with green beans
- Use in a dressing for a really good, herby potato salad with yoghurt dressing

Cheat's Preserved Lemons

When you haven't got the time (or lemons!) to make preserved lemons, you can very quickly and easily rustle up something similar that will work well enough for many recipes (including that on page 211).

2 lemons
3 tablespoons sugar
1 tablespoon salt
3 tablespoons lemon juice

Wash the lemons and cut them into halves and then quarters, then fine slices. Place them in a sterilised jar (page 232) and top with the sugar, salt and lemon juice. Shake well and seal. Use the next day. Store in the refrigerator.

Courgette, Ginger & Lemon Chutney

One of my favourite ways of using courgettes (zucchini), I'm never sure if this is a jam or a chutney, but it works in both sweet and savoury scenarios (with pancakes, or with cheese). The lemon is fundamental, which is partly why I wanted to include it in this book.

450 g (1 lb) prepared marrow
  or large courgettes (zucchini)
  (weight after de-seeding)
1 lemon
250 ml (8 fl oz/1 cup) water
250 g (9 oz/1¼ cups) caster
  (superfine) sugar
20 g (¾ oz) fresh root ginger,
  peeled and finely grated

Place a couple of saucers in the fridge to test the setting point later.

Top and tail the courgettes or marrows and cut in half lengthways. Scoop out the seeds and discard (or give to the chickens, if you happen to have one!). Cut the flesh (with the skin) into small pieces, about the size of a sugar cube.

Zest the lemon and set aside. Squeeze the juice and set aside. Place the squeezed halves in a muslin (cheesecloth) bag tied with string.

Place the courgettes or marrow in a pan with the water, cover, bring to a simmer and cook over a low heat, until translucent (this will take about 10 minutes)

Add the sugar, the grated lemon zest and juice, the grated ginger and the muslin bag with the lemon halves. Cook at a low simmer for 50–60 minutes, then test if it has reached setting point – dribble a little of the liquid onto one of the cold saucers, wait for 10 seconds and then push your finger through it. If you see wrinkles form then you have reached setting point. Keep cooking if there are no wrinkles and repeat the setting test as necessary.

Pour into the sterilised jars (page 232) and store for at least a few days (in a cool dark place) before opening.

Lemon Curd

MAKES 2–3
SMALL JARS
(350 ML/12 OZ)

The word curd is a wonderful one, the gentle purring 'currr' a soothing lullaby as you curl into a soft buttery bed, only to be slapped awake by the sharp sting of lemon and the thud of the final 'd'.

Like so many things in life, a good curd is about balance. Balance between thickness and dollop-ability, between sharpness and sweetness, between butter and eggs and enough lemon for all that fat not to overwhelm.

The consistency of this particular curd is just-set, quivering and timid as a church mouse, and its flavour is the perfect balance of sweet and sharp. It is wobbling and wonderful, primrose yellow and just translucent.

Lemon 'cheese', as it was originally known, first popped its yellow head up in recipe books of the 1800s, and it gave me great delight to read about it on the Italian Internet food-forum GialloZafferano, mentioned as an essential part of the 'unmissable English tea'. It reminded me poignantly of the first Christmas I spent in Sardinia. Under the tree were various unidentifiable objects wrapped up and labelled with my name. I opened them one by one. Every single one was a tea mug. I approached the last, which was slightly bigger than the rest. It was a tea mug and tea bags packaged together in a neat gift box. The extended family all looked slightly shifty and then burst out laughing.

I'm not sure how many English people still indulge in the 'unmissable English tea', which includes such delights as lemon curd and scones, but perhaps more of us should and the world would be a happier place. It's a tradition I am happy to bring to my Sardinian life. On winter Sundays we sometimes have an English tea, and perhaps I'll light the fire. There might be a Victoria sponge stuffed with whipped cream and lemon curd, too.

2 eggs plus 3 egg yolks
220 g (8 oz/1 cup plus
  2 tablespoons) sugar
finely grated zest of
  4–5 lemons
180 ml (6 fl oz/¾ cup) lemon
  juice
a good pinch of salt
150 g (5½ oz) butter, cubed

Whisk the eggs, egg yolks, sugar, zest and lemon juice in a bowl, then add the salt.

Transfer the mixture to a heavy-based saucepan over a very low heat and start whisking. Add the butter piece by piece, whisking all the time to incorporate. Keep whisking over a low heat until all of the butter has melted and the mixture begins to thicken to a custard consistency, making sure it is smooth and none of the egg begins to scramble.

Strain through a fine sieve into a bowl, then decant into sterilised jars (page 232).

Store in the refrigerator. Eat with a spoon when sad, on pancakes when happy, on toast for breakfast, in sandwiches with soft white bread. Or put inside a Victoria sponge and feel victorious.

Variations:

If you'd like to do a fragrant spin on the classic, I recommend adding a bay leaf (good for Christmas), a sprig or two of lavender or lemon verbena.

A *Lemon* IN THE HAND

Practical Uses

There is a good reason why so many cleaning products contain lemon in one form or another. With the power to provide perfume, actively remove odours, sterilise, kill bacteria and bleach, it is the original cleaner. It is a sort of chicken-and-egg dilemma, whether we associate the scent of lemon with cleanliness because we are used to it in our cleaning products, or if the scent of a lemon is inherently clean-smelling in itself. I think the latter. Either way, lemons are synonymous with cleaning and cleanliness.

BLEACHING, STAIN REMOVING & CLEANING

I have heard tell that some people use squeezed out lemon halves as washing up sponges, or at least toss them into their washing up water to both perfume it and help cut through grease.

A mixture of lemon juice and salt can be used for removing any stain from fabric, and for bleaching whites. Adding half a cup of lemon juice to a white wash helps whiten your whites. For stain removal, mix salt and lemon directly into a stain then leave it for half an hour and launder as usual.

A rough paste of lemon juice and salt is the ideal cleaner if you are lucky enough to own any copper pans or jelly moulds, and for shining many household metals. Scrub the paste in, then rinse off. A mixture of lemon juice and olive oil (one part lemon to two parts oil) can also be used to polish wooden furniture and keep it nourished. Washing your hands with lemon juice is also an excellent way to remove odours left by handling fish, garlic or other less agreeable smelling foods (this is not recommended if you have cuts on your hands!). Limonene, a component found in lemons and in lemon essential oil, is a natural solvent and this lemon oil can be used to clean kitchen and bathroom surfaces, as it dissolves dirt and grease.

PERFUME

The aromatic oils in lemon rind have the power to disguise other scents. Putting used lemon halves in the dishwasher stops it smelling of stale water or dirty plates; a lemon placed in a bowl of water and heated in the microwave for 30 seconds cleans the interior and leaves it smelling fresh; half a lemon in a bowl of water in the refrigerator does the same thing. Lemon essential oil is a wonderful thing to have in your home; add a few drops to an incense burner or add it to a spray bottle of water for your ironing or spritzing and perfuming home furnishings. In the summer months, pick some of your favourite flowers and float the flower heads in a bowl of fresh water scented with a few drops of lemon essential oil, like a sort of floating pot pourri.

DISINFECTING

Lemon is a natural disinfectant, and limonene has antibacterial properties. You can clean and disinfect chopping boards and surfaces with lemon juice.

About the Author

Letitia Clark is a food writer, illustrator and chef. After completing the Leiths diploma in food and wine she went on to work in some of London's top restaurants, including Spring, Morito and The Dock Kitchen.

She is the author of three cookbooks: *Bitter Honey* (2020), *La Vita è Dolce* (2021) and *Wild Figs and Fennel* (2024). She lives in Sardinia, where she writes, teaches and hosts cooking classes, as well as continuing her work as an illustrator.

Acknowledgements

Thanks are owed firstly to my family: to my mum, who inspired my love of lemons, and to my grandmother, who inspired my love of food in general, and who wielded that first Jif lemon so seductively over my childhood pancakes. To my dad, for having sherbert lemons in his glove compartment, and to my husband Lorenzo for traipsing around Amalfi with me and a small, hot, hungry child. Thanks, too, to said small child, AKA the Tiny Saint, for making the Amalfi trip such a memorable one – for both good and bad reasons – and for loving lemons as much as I do, including employing them as baby-sized footballs.

Thanks to the two Amalfi ladies who told me about their Lemon Moka.

Huge thanks to the team at Hardie Grant/Quadrille/Penguin Random House: Kajal Mistry, Eila Purvis and Judith Hannam, to editor Gillian Haslam and to designer Emma Wells.

Also, I would like to particularly thank Alice Adams Carosi, for making the shoot so wonderfully effortless and fun, and for bringing plenty of good sense, wisdom and good taste to the whole project. Alongside her was the brilliant and humble Benedetta Canale, whose eye for styling was pitch perfect, and who worked tirelessly and quietly, making everything so much more beautiful than I had dreamed of. Her choice of elephant songs was also much appreciated by smaller members of the team. The beauty of the dishes you see within these pages is entirely down to the prowess of these two women. May you both always be blessed with lemons.

Thanks to Casa Li Feruli, for providing the perfect shoot location in Sardinia (and all those amazing plates!).

Finally, enormous thanks to the inimitable Charlotte Bland, who worked her subtle magic once and again, and managed to capture the joy, serenity and beauty of the Sardinian Spring and its abundant lemons.

Index

A

almonds
  almond & lemon praline 142
  fried almond ravioli 168–9
  lemon, almond & mint pesto
    pasta 86
  lemon & almond layered
    celebration cake 138
  soft & chewy lemon & almond
    biscuits 120
  triflettes 144
Amalfi lemons 21, 24
amaretti biscuits
  triflettes 144
amaretto sour 229
anchovies
  baked red vegetables with lemon,
    anchovy & basil 38
  bruschetta with stracciatella &
    anchovies, confit tomatoes &
    lemon zest 48
  creamy fennel, lemon & pecorino
    bake 70
  rosemary, lemon & anchovy
    butter 196
  zesty salsa verde 204
Anderson, Hans Christian 8
Arcimboldo, Giuseppe 8
artichokes
  artichoke carbonara 75
  chicken braised with artichokes,
    saffron & lemon 102
  deep-fried artichokes with lemon
    pinwheels 42
asparagus
  burrata with lemony spring
    vegetables & pistachio pesto 47
Attlee, Helena 8–10

B

baking powder 32

basil
  baked red vegetables with lemon,
    anchovy & basil 38
  melon, lemon & basil sorbet 186
batter
  deep-fried artichokes with lemon
    pinwheels 42
biscuits
  ginger, honey & lemon brandy
    snaps 148
  lemon bars with polenta pastry &
    olive oil curd 122
  slightly salty lemon & lavender
    shortbread biscuits 125
  soft & chewy lemon & almond
    biscuits 120
brandy snaps
  ginger, honey & lemon brandy
    snaps 148
broad beans
  burrata with lemony spring
    vegetables & pistachio pesto 47
bruschetta with stracciatella &
  anchovies, confit tomatoes &
  lemon zest 48
buns
  lemon & elderflower iced buns
    126–7
burrata with lemony spring
  vegetables & pistachio pesto 47
butter
  lemon curd 236
  rosemary, lemon & anchovy
    butter 196

C

cabbage & kohlrabi salad with
  whole lemon, pecorino, chilli &
  pine nuts 62–3
cakes
  Allegra's whole lemon

ciambellone 150
  damp lemon, olive oil & fennel
    seed tea cake 132
  lemon & almond layered
    celebration cake 138
  lemon & coconut cream cake 136
  lemon, yoghurt & semolina cake
    with elderflower drizzle 135
cannellini beans
  double bean salad 60
  lemony minestra 64
capers
  double bean salad 60
  saffron tagliatelle with fresh
    tomato & lemon 72
  salt cod in spiced tomato sauce
    with capers & lemon 92
  spaghetti with tuna & lemons 78
  zesty salsa verde 204
caramel
  milk tart 158
cheese 32, 154
  artichoke carbonara 75
  baked sardines with lemon and
    Parmesan breadcrumbs 92
  bruschetta with stracciatella &
    anchovies, confit tomatoes &
    lemon zest 48
  burrata with lemony spring
    vegetables & pistachio pesto 47
  cabbage & kohlrabi salad with
    whole lemon, pecorino, chilli &
    pine nuts 62–3
  creamy fennel, lemon & pecorino
    bake 70
  creamy lemon linguine 77
  feta, lemon and melon salad 66
  fried cheese with lemon 44
  grilled/barbecued mozzarella in
    lemon leaves 108
  instant lemon & white chocolate
    mascarpone mousse 164

lemon, almond & mint pesto pasta 86

lemon & coconut cream cake 136

lemon & courgette carbonara 74–5

lemon & fennel risotto 89

lemon-marinated olives with feta & garlic 36

lemon tiramisù 167

pizzette with lemon, sausage and fennel 50

roasted lemon-leaf goat's cheese 110

Scotch ricotta 131

spring fregola salad 69

triflettes 144

chicken

baked, breadcrumbed lemon leaf chicken 112

chicken braised with artichokes, saffron & lemon 102

chicken, honey & preserved lemon tagine 98–9

chocolate

instant lemon & white chocolate mascarpone mousse 164

chutney

courgette, ginger & lemon chutney 235

citrons 15

coconut cream

lemon & coconut cream cake 136

coffee and lemon 18

espresso with lemon 218

courgettes

courgette, ginger & lemon chutney 235

feta, lemon and melon salad 66

lemon & courgette carbonara 74–5

lemony courgette scapece 59

lemony minestra 64

spring fregola salad 69

cream

almond, pistachio & lemon gelato 183

creamy fennel, lemon & pecorino bake 70

ginger, honey & lemon brandy snaps 148

instant lemon & white chocolate mascarpone mousse 164

lemon & almond layered celebration cake 138

lemon & elderflower iced buns 126–7

lemon panna cotta with strawberries 156

lemon possets in lemon boats 162

lemon-scented crema Catalana 161

lemon tiramisù 167

pavlova with lemon-olive oil curd 180

cucumber

feta, lemon and melon salad 66

custard

lemon custard ravioli 170

D

desserts

almond, pistachio & lemon gelato 183

fried almond ravioli 168–9

instant lemon & white chocolate mascarpone mousse 164

lazy lemon meringue pie 178

lemon & wild fennel sorbetto 184

lemon custard ravioli 170

lemon panna cotta with strawberries 156

lemon, pear & lemon verbena sorbet 190

lemon possets in lemon boats 162

lemon-scented crema Catalana 161

lemon self-saucing pudding 174

lemon tiramisù 167

melon, lemon & basil sorbet 186

milk tart 158

pavlova with lemon-olive oil curd 180

Sussex pond pudding 176

triflettes 144

dressings

lemony tahini dressing 198

preserved lemon & herb yoghurt dressing 211

drinks

amaretto sour 229

coffee and lemon 18

espresso with lemon 218

lavender & honey lemonade 216

rose & raspberry lemonade 226

E

eggs

almond, pistachio & lemon gelato 183

classic crêpes 130

double bean salad 60

fried almond ravioli 168–9

lazy lemon meringue pie 178

lemon bars with polenta pastry & olive oil curd 122

lemon curd 236

lemon custard ravioli 170

lemon-scented crema Catalana 161

milk tart 158

Scotch ricotta 131

elderflower blossom

lemon, yoghurt & semolina cake with elderflower drizzle 135

elderflower cordial

lemon & elderflower iced buns 126–7

equipment 28

F

fennel
creamy fennel, lemon & pecorino bake 70
lemon & fennel pork meatballs 104
lemon & fennel risotto 89
lemon & wild fennel sorbetto 184
lemony fennel & potato purée 200
pizzette with lemon, sausage and fennel 50
shaved fennel & lemon salad 56
fennel seeds
damp lemon, olive oil & fennel seed tea cake 132
feta
feta, lemon and melon salad 66
lemon-marinated olives with feta & garlic 36
fish 153
baked red vegetables with lemon, anchovy & basil 38
baked sardines with lemon and Parmesan breadcrumbs 92
bruschetta with stracciatella & anchovies, confit tomatoes & lemon zest 48
creamy fennel, lemon & pecorino bake 70
rosemary, lemon & anchovy butter 196
sea bass carpaccio with citrus 90
spaghetti with tuna & lemons 78
zesty salsa verde 204
fregola
spring fregola salad 69
fruit 154

G

garlic
lemon-marinated olives with feta & garlic 36

ginger
courgette, ginger & lemon chutney 235
ginger, honey & lemon brandy snaps 148
goat's cheese
roasted lemon-leaf goat's cheese 110
green beans
double bean salad 60
gremolata 208

H

Hazan, Marcella 10
herbs
preserved lemon & herb yoghurt dressing 211
zesty salsa verde 204
history of lemons 15–17
honey
espresso with lemon 218
lavender & honey lemonade 216

I

ingredients 32

K

kohlrabi
cabbage & kohlrabi salad with whole lemon, pecorino, chilli & pine nuts 62–3

L

lavender
lavender & honey lemonade 216
slightly salty lemon & lavender shortbread biscuits 125
lemon curd 236

lazy lemon meringue pie 178
lemon tiramisù 167
pavlova with lemon-olive oil curd 180
lemon flowers 193
lemon juice 213
amaretto sour 229
classic crêpes 130
double bean salad 60
grilled squid 96
lemon & elderflower iced buns 126–7
lemon bars with polenta pastry & olive oil curd 122
lemon, pear & lemon verbena sorbet 190
lemon possets in lemon boats 162
lemon tiramisù 167
lemony tahini dressing 198
melon, lemon & basil sorbet 186
salt cod in spiced tomato sauce with capers & lemon 92
sea bass carpaccio with citrus 90
lemon leaves
almond & lemon praline 142
baked, breadcrumbed lemon leaf chicken 112
grilled/barbecued mozzarella in lemon leaves 108
roasted lemon-leaf goat's cheese 110
lemon oil 223, 224, 240
lemon verbena leaves
lemon, pear & lemon verbena sorbet 190
lemon zest 153–4
bruschetta with stracciatella & anchovies, confit tomatoes & lemon zest 48
espresso with lemon 218
feta, lemon and melon salad 66
fried almond ravioli 168–9

gremolata 208

instant lemon & white chocolate mascarpone mousse 164

lemon & coconut cream cake 136

lemon & wild fennel sorbetto 184

lemon custard ravioli 170

lemon-scented crema Catalana 161

milk tart 158

pizzette with lemon, sausage and fennel 50

slightly salty lemon & lavender shortbread biscuits 125

soft & chewy lemon & almond biscuits 120

lemonade

lavender & honey lemonade 216

rose & raspberry lemonade 226

lemons

Amalfi lemons 21, 24

cleaning properties 239–40

composition of 223

in culture and cooking 17, 203, 213

history 15–17

medicinal uses 224–5

Sorreto lemons 18–21

lemons, preserved

cheat's preserved lemons 234

chicken, honey & preserved lemon tagine 98–9

preserved lemon & herb yoghurt dressing 211

proper preserved lemons 232

lemons (recipes)

Allegra's whole lemon ciambellone 150

almond, pistachio & lemon gelato 183

artichoke carbonara 75

baked, breadcrumbed lemon leaf chicken 112

baked red vegetables with lemon, anchovy & basil 38

baked sardines with lemon and Parmesan breadcrumbs 92

burrata with lemony spring vegetables & pistachio pesto 47

cabbage & kohlrabi salad with whole lemon, pecorino, chilli & pine nuts 62–3

chicken, honey & preserved lemon tagine 98–9

coffee and lemon 18

courgette, ginger & lemon chutney 235

creamy fennel, lemon & pecorino bake 70

creamy lemon linguine 77

damp lemon, olive oil & fennel seed tea cake 132

deep-fried artichokes with lemon pinwheels 42

ginger, honey & lemon brandy snaps 148

lavender & honey lemonade 216

lazy lemon meringue pie 178

lemon, almond & mint pesto pasta 86

lemon & almond layered celebration cake 138

lemon & courgette carbonara 74–5

lemon & fennel pork meatballs 104

lemon & fennel risotto 89

lemon curd 236

lemon-marinated olives with feta & garlic 36

lemon panna cotta with strawberries 156

lemon self-saucing pudding 174

lemon, yoghurt & semolina cake with elderflower drizzle 135

lemony courgette scapece 59

lemony fennel & potato purée 200

lemony minestra 64

prawn, chilli & lemon zest linguine 84–5

preserved lemon & herb yoghurt dressing 211

roasted lemon-leaf goat's cheese 110

rose & raspberry lemonade 226

rosemary, lemon & anchovy butter 196

saffron tagliatelle with fresh tomato & lemon 72

shaved fennel & lemon salad 56

spaghetti with tuna & lemons 78

spring fregola salad 69

Sussex pond pudding 176

zesty salsa verde 204

limonene 223, 239, 240

linguine

creamy lemon linguine 77

prawn, chilli & lemon zest linguine 84–5

M

mascarpone

creamy lemon linguine 77

instant lemon & white chocolate mascarpone mousse 164

lemon & coconut cream cake 136

lemon tiramisù 167

meatballs

lemon & fennel pork meatballs 104

melon

feta, lemon and melon salad 66

melon, lemon & basil sorbet 186

meringues

lazy lemon meringue pie 178

pavlova with lemon-olive oil curd 180

milk

lemon custard ravioli 170

milk tart 158

mozzarella

grilled/barbecued mozzarella in lemon leaves 108
pizzette with lemon, sausage and fennel 50

N

Neruda, Pablo 10

O

olive oil 32
    damp lemon, olive oil & fennel seed tea cake 132
    lemon bars with polenta pastry & olive oil curd 122
    pavlova with lemon-olive oil curd 180
olives
    lemon-marinated olives with feta & garlic 36

P

pancakes
    classic crêpes 130
    Scotch ricotta 131
Parmesan
    baked sardines with lemon and Parmesan breadcrumbs 92
    lemon & fennel risotto 89
parsley
    gremolata 208
pasta
    artichoke carbonara 75
    creamy lemon linguine 77
    lemon, almond & mint pesto pasta 86
    lemon & courgette carbonara 74–5
    lemony minestra 64
    prawn, chilli & lemon zest linguine 84–5

saffron tagliatelle with fresh tomato & lemon 72
spaghetti with tuna & lemons 78
spring fregola salad 69
pavlova with lemon-olive oil curd 180
pears
    lemon, pear & lemon verbena sorbet 190
peas
    burrata with lemony spring vegetables & pistachio pesto 47
    lemony minestra 64
    spring fregola salad 69
pecorino 32
    artichoke carbonara 75
    cabbage & kohlrabi salad with whole lemon, pecorino, chilli & pine nuts 62–3
    creamy fennel, lemon & pecorino bake 70
    creamy lemon linguine 77
    fried cheese with lemon 44
    lemon, almond & mint pesto pasta 86
    lemon & courgette carbonara 74–5
    pizzette with lemon, sausage and fennel 50
pectin 223
peppers
    baked red vegetables with lemon, anchovy & basil 38
pesto
    burrata with lemony spring vegetables & pistachio pesto 47
    lemon, almond & mint pesto pasta 86
pine nuts
    cabbage & kohlrabi salad with whole lemon, pecorino, chilli & pine nuts 62–3
pistachios

almond, pistachio & lemon gelato 183
burrata with lemony spring vegetables & pistachio pesto 47
pizzette with lemon, sausage and fennel 50
polenta pastry
    lemon bars with polenta pastry & olive oil curd 122
pork
    lemon & fennel pork meatballs 104
potatoes
    lemony fennel & potato purée 200
praline
    almond & lemon praline 142
prawn, chilli & lemon zest linguine 84–5
preserved lemons
    cheat's preserved lemons 234
    chicken, honey & preserved lemon tagine 98–9
    preserved lemon & herb yoghurt dressing 211
    proper preserved lemons 232

R

raspberries
    instant lemon & white chocolate mascarpone mousse 164
    rose & raspberry lemonade 226
    triflettes 144
ravioli
    fried almond ravioli 168–9
    lemon custard ravioli 170
rice
    lemon & fennel risotto 89
ricotta
    Scotch ricotta 131
    spring fregola salad 69

triflettes 144

risotto
    lemon & fennel risotto 89

rocket
    cabbage & kohlrabi salad with whole lemon, pecorino, chilli & pine nuts 62–3
    double bean salad 60
    spaghetti with tuna & lemons 78

rose & raspberry lemonade 226

rosemary, lemon & anchovy butter 196

S

saffron
    chicken braised with artichokes, saffron & lemon 102
    chicken, honey & preserved lemon tagine 98–9
    saffron tagliatelle with fresh tomato & lemon 72

salads 213
    cabbage & kohlrabi salad with whole lemon, pecorino, chilli & pine nuts 62–3
    double bean salad 60
    feta, lemon and melon salad 66
    lemony courgette scapece 59
    shaved fennel & lemon salad 56
    spring fregola salad 69

salsa verde
    zesty salsa verde 204

salt cod in spiced tomato sauce with capers & lemon 92

sardines
    baked sardines with lemon and Parmesan breadcrumbs 92

sausages
    pizzette with lemon, sausage and fennel 50

scurvy 224

sea bass carpaccio with citrus 90

seasoning 203, 213

semolina
    lemon, yoghurt & semolina cake with elderflower drizzle 135

sorbet
    lemon & wild fennel sorbetto 184

Sorreto lemons 18–21

soup/broth
    lemony minestra 64

spaghetti with tuna & lemons 78

squid
    grilled squid 96

stracciatella
    bruschetta with stracciatella & anchovies, confit tomatoes & lemon zest 48

strawberries
    lemon & almond layered celebration cake 138
    lemon panna cotta with strawberries 156

T

tagliatelle
    saffron tagliatelle with fresh tomato & lemon 72

tahini
    lemony tahini dressing 198

tomatoes
    baked red vegetables with lemon, anchovy & basil 38
    bruschetta with stracciatella & anchovies, confit tomatoes & lemon zest 48
    double bean salad 60
    prawn, chilli & lemon zest linguine 84–5
    saffron tagliatelle with fresh tomato & lemon 72
    salt cod in spiced tomato sauce with capers & lemon 92

tuna
    spaghetti with tuna & lemons 78

V

vegetables 55, 213
    burrata with lemony spring vegetables & pistachio pesto 47

vinaigrette
    double bean salad 60

W

Woolf, Virginia 8

Y

yoghurt
    lemon, yoghurt & semolina cake with elderflower drizzle 135
    pavlova with lemon-olive oil curd 180
    preserved lemon & herb yoghurt dressing 211